LEGALISING DRUGS
Debates and dilemmas

Philip Bean

CLACKAMAS COMMUNITY COLLEGE LIBRARY PROPERTY

D0556297

First published in Great Britain in 2010 by

The Policy Press
University of Bristol
Fourth Floor, Beacon House
Queen's Road
Bristol BS8 1QU

t: +44 (0)117 331 4054
f: +44 (0)117 331 4093
e: tpp-info@bristol.ac.uk
www.policypress.co.uk

North American office:
The Policy Press
c/o International Specialized Books Services
920 NE 58th Avenue, Suite 300
Portland,
OR 97213-3786, USA
t: +1 503 287 3093
f: +1 503 280 8832
e: info@isbs.com

© The Policy Press 2010

British Library Cataloguing in Publication Data
A catalogue record for this book is available from the British Library.

Library of Congress Cataloging-in-Publication Data
A catalog record for this book has been requested.

ISBN 978 1 84742 375 7 paperback

The right of Philip Bean to be identified as author of this work has been asserted by him in accordance with the 1988 Copyright, Designs and Patents Act.

All rights reserved: no part of this publication may be reproduced, stored in a retrieval system, or transmitted in any form or by any means, electronic, mechanical, photocopying, recording, or otherwise without the prior permission of The Policy Press.

The statements and opinions contained within this publication are solely those of the author and not of the University of Bristol or The Policy Press. The University of Bristol and The Policy Press disclaim responsibility for any injury to persons or property resulting from any material published in this publication.

The Policy Press works to counter discrimination on grounds of gender, race, disability, age and sexuality.

Cover design by The Policy Press
Printed and bound in Great Britain by Cromwell Press Group, Trowbridge

For Phoebe Enola

Contents

Preface

This book has grown out of a chapter I wrote for a third edition of a text entitled *Drugs and Crime* (Bean, 2008), the chapter a response to a stinging criticism from a reviewer who thought that there was something amiss with an earlier edition, which did not examine the justification for linking drugs to crime. Meeting that criticism led to a greater awareness of the subject matter, which has grown and developed over time. Yet when I looked closely at the literature, it was astonishing that in spite of public concern about the drugs problem, and many suggestions to solve it, little real interest has been shown in the UK in what can be called the 'legalisation debate'. Hopefully this short book will remedy that and provoke further interest.

Another difficulty has been the lack of an agreed or accepted definition for many of the terms. For example, 'legalisation' is often used to include proposals in opposition to current government policy, while 'prohibition' has begun to mean more than controlling drugs through the law, and to include 'decriminalisation', which is also used in the debates about changing the classification of drugs such as cannabis. Or it has come to approximate to 'medicalisation', meaning the supply of drugs by and through the medical profession. And this on top of the initial problems of defining a 'drug'. In what follows, I have tried to be rather more precise, trying to impose some order on what is often a chaotic use of language, but not always succeeding in that sometimes it has been convenient to refer to legalisation and prohibition in the same form as above.

The aim throughout is theoretical, not empirical, although I shall draw on the empirical literature where appropriate. I want to examine some of the proposals surrounding the 'legalisation debate' and do so with reference to the literature. Some clarification is needed about what is considered. First to say what is not. I have not dealt with that part of the debate centring on the proscription of drugs in certain types of employment, or the use of drug tests to determine drug use, or the offence of driving under the influence

—

of drugs. I assume that no one disputes that driving or flying an aeroplane under the influence of drugs, or being under the influence in similarly hazardous occupations, should continue to be prohibited. I have accordingly seen these matters as outside the scope of this enquiry. That does not mean that they should be ignored; there are important sociological and jurisprudential issues to be considered, especially over the use of imposed drug tests, but I have seen these as outside the boundaries of this debate. What is included are the various proposals centring around the control, possession and supply of selected regulated substances, which for convenience largely means those covered by the 1971 Misuse of Drugs Act.

Another difficulty has been the shortage of British literature, and what there is has produced a lopsided approach, largely dominated by harm reduction. Not entirely, however, as some commentators have sought a wider view. Nonetheless, that has meant I have had to look elsewhere, mainly to the US, where the debate has been more intense. That adds to the complications, as differences between the policies of the two countries needs to be acknowledged, not the least that the UK has not gone down 'the war on drugs' route with all that entails. Also, the 'British system' can be said to prohibit the use of drugs but also permit certain drugs such as heroin to be prescribed whether for terminal conditions by a registered physician, or by certain selected licensed physicians in the treatment of addiction.

Outside government circles there has rarely been anyone in the UK prepared to defend current practices, but the government has set itself defiantly against those seeking change. It claims to have massive public support. However, there have been challenges to established orthodoxies and I have tried to include those – these orthodoxies incidentally do not always favour full-scale prohibition.

I have set out the book in ways that I hope will assist anyone wanting to pick their way through a swathe of proposals, nearly all covering the same ground yet often from different standpoints. Repetition is, I fear, endemic.Everyone has a view about the links between drugs and crime and about the future were their proposals to be accepted. All are optimistic. Similarly, everyone claims that

—

their proposals will solve the drugs problem and make life better for everybody, the drug user and non-user alike. I have wanted to subject these proposals to scrutiny, to see what would be achieved were such proposals to be accepted and point out the strengths and weaknesses therein. In the final chapter I have set out five questions that I think a rational drugs policy must answer.

I want to give special thanks to Leo Goodman and Joy Mott for making valuable comments throughout. They gave considerable time and thought to the various drafts and over a lengthy period of time, for which I am very grateful. Needless to say, any errors that remain are mine.

Philip Bean
March 2009

1

Introduction

When asked how best to proceed with regard to the drug problem, Mark Kleiman (2008) said that there were things that we could do about drug policy that would reduce the numbers in prison, and the extent of drug abuse and drug-related crime, but legalisation was not one of them. Why? Because, he said, there was no public support for it, and anyway he thought that the legalisation debate was a distraction from doing the real work of fixing the drug problem. Distraction or not, for some it is an immediate and pressing matter. They see legalisation as the way out of a policy failure, the more optimistic believing that it is only a matter of time before the government realises its error. These include Richard Brunstrom, Chief Constable of North Wales, who said on a BBC News programme (1 January 2008) that it was inevitable that drugs would be legalised in the next 10 years. He acknowledged that his views were not popular, and indeed senior figures elsewhere endorsed that, saying that there was no inevitability about legalisation, but he firmly believed that public attitudes were changing.

He is not alone. Julian Critchley, a former senior civil servant who was responsible for coordinating the government's anti-drugs policy, now says that legalisation would be less harmful than the current strategy and that his views are shared by the 'overwhelming majority' of professionals in the field, including police officers, health workers and members of the government (*The Guardian*, 13 August 2008). But how realistic are such hopes when faced with stern refusals from the government to change policy? Governments can of course change their minds, and sometimes do, but the point is forcibly made by the present government that it has no wish to alter course. Why? Because it says that the current system works: 'The fact that drugs are illegal deters people from misuse and limits experimentation. The Law also provides opportunities through the

Criminal Justice System to identify and engage drug-using offenders in treatment' (House of Commons Home Affairs Select Committee, 2002a). In this it finds support from some international organisations. The United Nations Office on Drugs and Crime (UNODC, 2007, para 25) has said that member states must have the will to commit themselves to drug control, a view also shared by the President of the International Narcotics Control Board who called legalisation 'simplistic and misplaced' because 'it ignored historical facts' (INCB, 2008, Foreword).

Of course, the opponents of prohibition have the advantage, it being always easier to attack than defend, and in this case the prohibitionists offer them an easy target, often failing to provide a convincing case for continuance. And the legalisers are protected in another sense, for there are no full-scale legalisation experiments being undertaken, only some in favour of harm reduction, or medicalisation, or occasionally decriminalisation, as with cannabis. Yet prohibitionists can always resort to the populist nature of their policy. James Inciardi (1999) makes the point for them. He says of America that an overwhelming majority of the population, including their political representatives, as well as researchers and clinicians working in the drugs field, consider legalisation to be simplistic and dangerous. And he notes that by contrast a small but highly vocal and prestigious minority argue that the benefits of legalising drugs are well worth the risk (1999, p 55).

The debate in the UK has often been stylised with that 'small but highly vocal minority' having the advantage of the publicity. Not always of course: governments too have their media outlets, but those who chatter most – the journalists, policy analysts etc – are almost always on the side of change. And change invariably means some form of legalisation. In an exasperated moment against that 'highly vocal prestigious minority', Kim Howells (*The Times*, 2008) the then Foreign Office Minister, reportedly said, 'It is not enough to assume that if you eat muesli and go to first nights of Harold Pinter that the drug barons in Afghanistan are going to go away.'

–

2

The shortage of experimental data has placed limitations on the quality of the debate. The prohibitionists cannot prove they are right, but their opponents are not able to prove they are wrong. This has led Arnold Trebach (quoted in Husak, 1992, pp 214-15) to suggest that the way to proceed is to experiment in various stages, eventually leading to full legalisation, but opting for an incremental approach. Apart from the difficulty of setting up these experimental stages – I doubt that many governments would be interested – the data will certainly be biased or distorted. For example, were those experiments to allow drugs to be more easily obtained, users outside that catchment area might be attracted to it. An exodus of Canadian addicts to Britain in the 1960s is testimony to this. So too, an experiment decriminalising certain drugs, say cannabis, might produce the same problems, as critics of the Dutch coffee shops have maintained, where new users or those outside the geographical area are attracted to that area.

There is no shortage of opinions about how best to proceed, yet behind many proposals lie deeper issues, often moral, social and political but sometimes about fashion, lifestyle or outcome. Proposals for future policy are promoted as much by values as by estimated consequences (Moore, 1992b, p 136). Occasionally, the debate is as about the very soul of society. James Inciardi (1999, p 55) exemplifies this when he sees opposition to prohibition coming from that highly vocal but prestigious minority who argue that legalising drugs is worth the risk. He doubts that it is, believing that legalisation would undermine the integrity of our society. Inciardi and McBride (1989, p 279) say that it will bear most heavily on the poorest members of society, especially those within minority ethnic communities who are among the heaviest users. They also fear letting the genie out of the bottle as re-prohibition is no easy option. Other supporters of prohibition present their resistance to change in equally moral terms, such as 'stopping the flood gates opening' or 'not wanting to go soft on offenders', or more importantly, in terms of fears of encouraging irresponsibility, and promoting a society that becomes increasingly dysfunctional. They echo William Bennett, the US Drug Czar, who said that drug use destroys human character, dignity and autonomy, as well as burning away a sense of responsibility (Bennett, 1989). Ethan Nadelmann (1999b, p 31) disagrees, saying that the most unfortunate victims of prohibition are not the drug users but the law-abiding residents of America's ghettos, for they have had to put up with the large numbers of ghetto dwellers who have become drug users, and with the dealers and all that drug abuse means within these slum communities. In a field with so many conflicts and polar opposites, it is not surprising that the reconciliation of basic views is well-nigh impossible.

Those seeking change are often no less full of zeal. To some, prohibition represents an imposition on citizens by preventing a recreational activity, which may be harmful to the user. Others are concerned that prohibition is wasteful of resources. But always, the centre of the argument is about crime, illegal drug markets and the cost of enforcement. All agree that prohibition is a failure; they point to the large numbers of users and cite the high levels of crime associated with current policy. Picking ones way through these various positions is difficult enough, made worse by the way the debate has become increasingly politicised, often with more than a shade of self-righteousness attached, all to the detriment of its quality.

Models and ideal types

In practice, most governments adopt a mixture of policies, while retaining one as dominant. In the UK, the emphasis is on prohibition, but running alongside are others, some integral, some less so. Harm reduction plays an important part in government thinking; so too does medicalisation where it is still possible for heroin addicts to receive maintenance supplies; as does decriminalisation, which is aimed at reducing penalties. For convenience and in order to produce a rather enforced and artificial clarity, I have posited prohibition as the only government position. This is not entirely true of course and where it distorts the evidence I have pointed to that.

–

What I have tried to do is to present the various policy options as ideal types, of which I have selected six. These are:

- prohibition
- harm reduction
- medicalisation
- decriminalisation
- legal moralism
- economic liberalism

I have placed these ideal types on a spectrum moving in the direction of increased availability (Kleiman and Saiger, 1990, p 541). So, prohibition is at one end and economic liberalism is at the other. In between, and located at various points on the spectrum, are harm reduction, medicalisation, and decriminalisation with harm reduction most closely allied to prohibition. I recognise that these ideal types may not conform to everyone's vision of the complexity of the debate, but this seems to me the most appropriate way forward.

Imposing some order on the terminology is also difficult. Starting with prohibition, an adequate if not entirely satisfactory definition is the imposition of legal restrictions on the possession and use of selected substances. These include the substances controlled under the 1971 Misuse of Drugs Act and the pharmacy and poisons legislation, as well as that limiting the sale and distribution of alcohol and tobacco. In practice, I shall reserve the debate for the possession and supply of those substances controlled under the 1971 Misuse of Drugs Act. I shall refer to those listed substances as 'drugs', and do so aware that this too is an unsatisfactory term, but is nonetheless convenient.[1] 'Legalisation' is used throughout; I have used it as a generic term, covering a wide range of activities, but referring to any proposal which seeks to amend or repeal existing legislation. Again, not entirely satisfactory, but many opponents of current policy call themselves 'legalisers' when they want little more than amendments to the legislation, or see themselves opposed to particular government decisions. Others want more radical change.

Moving along the spectrum to 'harm reduction', I use the definition provided by the International Harm Reduction Association (1996, p 1) as 'policies and programmes which attempt primarily to reduce the adverse health, social and economic consequences of mood altering substances to individual drug users, their families and their communities'. 'Medicalisation' is no less complicated but as used here means the provision of controlled drugs through medical and allied services. 'Decriminalisation' is more difficult: I have used it as including policies aimed at reducing the legal sanctions of specific drugs and/or reducing the severity of the sentence. Reducing cannabis from a Class B drug to a Class C drug with lower criminal penalties would be a typical decriminalisation proposal.

At the far end of the spectrum is a disparate group of proposals in which supporters aim to remove most if not all legal restrictions on those proscribed substances. These include economic liberals such as Milton Friedman. There are others, such as Thomas Szasz, who also have a great deal in common with legal moralists who challenge the right of the state to punish adults who use drugs recreationally. For example, the organisation *Liberty*, in its evidence to the House of Commons Home Affairs Select Committee (Liberty, 2001), argued that recreational drug use was primarily self-harming, causing limited harm to others, and on the basis of protecting our freedoms it was no business of the state to intervene.

Presented in this stark form, no account is taken of the various subdivisions in these ideal types.[2] Some legalisers at one end of the spectrum want to replace existing controls with something akin to the pharmacy and poisons control model. Richard Stevenson (1994, p 62), for example, says that 'Sales would be restricted to pharmacists, and Governments would insist on licensing producers.' Others want a supply system similar to that for alcohol (Trebach and Inciardi, 1993, p 80). Still others aim for the elimination of government intervention throughout the drug market, including alcohol (Thornton, 1998) while Milton Friedman accepts the free market philosophy but wants to prohibit the sale of alcohol to certain groups (Friedman and Szasz, 1992, p 655). Some medicalisers want to provide heroin substitutes such

–

6

as methadone to heroin users, and some want medical prescribing as is current policy in the UK, while others commend prescribing users their drug of choice.

What of harm reduction? Some want to reduce the number of harms, others want to reduce a selected few, and still others want a more inclusive approach, which is to provide benefits. Finally, decriminalisation; this may involve changes in levels of legal severity, or it may involve removing certain drugs or activities altogether from legal control. All this makes for a rather messy debate, but regrettably that cannot be helped.

Methodology and utilitarianism

I want to make two points before proceeding further. First, although many commentators have expressed views about prohibition, I have not been able to include all of them. I have selected those that appear to be the most prominent. Again, my selection is personal and may not please everyone, but those selected appear to me to have made a contribution to the debate. My aim is to open up the argument, leaving it to others to delve more deeply into its complexity.

Second, a great deal of the debate centres around harm and the prevention of harm. By implication this means that the debate is conducted in utilitarian terms although rarely acknowledged as such. In traditional utilitarian style, proposals presented are aimed at promoting happiness, or if not, then preventing harm.[3] Prohibitionists and their opponents have used similar utilitarian arguments when considering imposing legal controls; prohibitionists say that control prevents drug use (creates happiness), opponents say that it makes things worse (creates harms). Or, again, prohibitionists justify control by reference to the likely social consequences of legalisation, pointing to the possible increase in drug use, and the impact that would have on society. In typical Benthamite fashion, critics of prohibition say that it produces crime, and in greater amounts than the laws prevent. Or that the impurities in the drugs as a result of prohibition create more harms. These are typical, one might almost say classical, utilitarian arguments.

The solutions are also typically utilitarian. Those suggesting that drugs should be provided on prescription do so in the same utilitarian language, that is, that were more drugs to be purchased legally, or prescribed by physicians, then harms would decrease. Proposals to decriminalise drugs appear in similar fashion; reclassifying cannabis from a Class B to a Class C drug will, it is said, reduce the penalties for law-abiding citizens and so promote fewer harms. Leave it as a Class B drug and it will reduce respect for the criminal justice system. I do not want to make too much of this classical portrayal of a well-established debate, yet the way it has been presented makes it difficult to ignore. Even in a veiled form, utilitarianism emerges, and as a veiled utilitarian myself, with strong sympathies to John Stuart Mill, I have no difficulty with that approach. The point I want to make is that the utilitarian format dominates; it does so in distinct ways, whether in the manner in which the debate has been conducted, or in the manner in which I have interpreted the debate. Not entirely, but sufficiently so to point to a pronounced utilitarian influence throughout.

A summary of the content

The format for the book is that it divides neatly into two parts. In the first part – Chapters Two and Three – I set out the ideal types and their strengths and weaknesses. In the second part – Chapters Four, Five and Six – I examine some of the implications of what is being suggested. In more detail the chapters are as follows. In Chapter Two I examine the more radical proposals set out as ideal types. That means determining first what is meant by prohibition, then contrasting this with economic liberalism, and setting both against a rights-based argument from the legal moralists, the central feature being that adults have a moral right to use recreational drugs, and it is no business of governments to take that away. In Chapter Three I deal with other ideal types where measures are less radical and more reformist and which include harm reduction, medicalisation and decriminalisation, although the proposal by the Transform Drug Policy Foundation borders more on the radical as it offers change from one control system to another.

–

I have nonetheless retained it within the reformist perspective, as it seems less radical than others. In these chapters the aim is to open out the discussion, without taking a particular stance but listing some of the more prominent criticisms. I begin the second part of the book with Chapter Four where I examine the problem of crime, and then I move on to the special problems of juveniles in Chapter Five. In Chapter Six I look at the impact on the community and the individual users and examine the commercial systems that might follow legalisation. Finally in Chapter 7, entitled 'Some concluding thoughts', I make an assessment of the main arguments, illustrating five questions that any rational drug policy ought to answer. This is not as a way of coming to conclusions, but as a way of suggesting the strengths and weaknesses of the various propositions and pointing to the future.

Notes

[1] I have used the terms 'users' and 'addicts' interchangeably. It is difficult to avoid such terminology as it is used throughout most proposals.

[2] To give an example of the level of confusion that can sometimes arise, a view was put forward at a fringe meeting of the 2006 Liberal Democrats conference where Mr C. Davies, an MEP, argued for a form of legalisation, which he did not make clear, or describe how it would operate, but he believed it would 'contribute to harm reduction, tackle gun culture, save police time and reduce the amount of drug-related crime including theft' (*BBC News*, 18 September 2006). He then added almost as an afterthought: 'But also people should have the freedom to put into their bodies what they want without any more harm than they would want' (*BBC News*, 18 September 2006).

[3] Utilitarianism is not without its problems. One that has plagued utilitarianism throughout and is present here is a definitional problem; what after all is meant by 'harm'? What produces harm, and how is it measured? Are harms to self as important as harms to others? Are harms to be considered alongside benefits and, if so, which is the more important? Once benefits are introduced, the argument becomes more

9

complex; how to identify them and set them against harms? For example, to say that inappropriate laws produce harm, and appropriate laws produce benefits, is difficult to calculate. Or, that prescribing heroin as maintenance will promote benefits. This again is difficult to calculate, not the least because there is no experiment by which to conduct the evaluation, only the prescribing practices of the 1960s. Or, finally, that the harm suffered by the legal punishments outweighs the harm from taking drugs. Perhaps yes for those serving long sentences, but difficult to assess where the health of the users is included.

The traditional clash between utilitarianism and rights theorists also shows itself. To the rights theorists, utilitarianism has little to offer, and much to reject. Utilitarians have little to say about natural rights, liberty, justice, or the impact of drug use on individual freedoms. After all, Bentham (Bentham, 1948, pp 240-1) called justice 'an imaginary personage fit only for the convenience of discourse' and natural rights as 'nonsense on stilts'. That legacy remains. It shows itself in numerous ways in the debate, especially in the discussion on the right of adults to use a recreational drug. 'Rights' sit uneasily aside discussions on harm reduction.

2

Prohibition, economic liberalism and legal moralism

Prohibition

In the first part of this book, I want to begin with prohibition, which is the major policy of choice in the UK, and in almost all other countries. A workmanlike definition, useful at this stage, is the imposition of legal restrictions on the use of selected substances. Prohibition restricts production and possession, and makes unlawful the distribution of certain substances without proper authority. Under the 1971 Misuse of Drugs Act, the major piece of legislation, drugs are classified according to the extent of harms they present, there being three classes; Class A providing the maximum penalties, and Class C the minimum. Of course, prohibition in the UK is more complicated than this, involving numerous policies and programmes, some of which include the ideal types described in Chapter One, but many do not. The drugs controlled under the 1971 Misuse of Drugs Act represent a small proportion of all the drugs sold as proprietary medicines or prescribed for medical purposes, all of which fall within the prohibition remit. The former are given prominence, the latter ignored. To concentrate on selected drugs such as heroin or cocaine distorts the picture, yet these have dominated the discussion, and for these purposes the 1971 Act will be the focus of the debate.

Prohibition derives from the 1961 UN Single Convention, the 1971 Convention on Psychotropic Substances and the 1988 Convention against the Illicit Traffic in Narcotic Drugs, and is in part justified because the UK is a signatory to these conventions. The requirements of the conventions are to control the manufacture,

possession and import of certain drugs, although each country has
some latitude as to how it goes about things. I do not want to make
too much of this, but it remains a point worth noting. It would be
extremely difficult, but not impossible, for the UK to unravel its
international obligations, although Richard Stevenson (1994, p 60)
says that 'It is unlikely the UK would remain alone for long.' Since
1912, the problem of drug addiction has been seen to require an
international response, and that position remains. (See Bean, 1974, for
a discussion on how drugs such as cannabis were first included under
the 1920 Dangerous Drugs Act.) The UK's obligations were clarified
by the House of Commons Home Affairs Committee (2002a, para
265), which stated: 'The UK is one of many signatories to several
International treaties on drugs, which constitute a fairly restrictive
cradle around our own legislative regime.' A critic, Lord Mancroft
in the House of Lords, argued that 'we as a nation – partly because of
the UN [United Nations] treaties – devote far too much time, money
and effort to the failed policy of trying to reduce supply and do not
spend enough resources, effort, time, money and concentration on
trying to reduce demand' (House of Lords, 22 January 2009, col
1804, *Hansard*).

In the Second Reading of the 1971 Misuse of Drugs Act, Lord
Windlesham, the then Minister of State for the Home Office,
provided an official definition of prohibition, amounting almost to
a justification (*Hansard*, 14 February 1971). He said that the guiding
principle in the government's mind was that society has a right to
use the criminal law to protect itself from forces that may threaten
its existence as a politically, socially or economically viable order.
He added that there was popular support for this principle, as most
people would agree that there should be safeguards restricting the
production and supply of potent medicines and drugs that are taken
for non-medical purposes. Lord Windelsham again: 'We cannot
stand by and watch appalled and uncomprehending while a disabling
and unnatural habit flourishes in our society' (*Hansard*, 14 February
1971). Or this time in the government's reply to the Third Report
of the Home Affairs Committee:

Drugs are responsible for the undermining of family and community life. The misery drug misuse causes cannot be underestimated. Drug misuse destroys the lives of individuals, families and communities. It destroys potential, and hope, and preys on the most vulnerable – from devastated countries like Afghanistan to the poorest in the UK, and on our most vulnerable young people. Drug misuse contributes dramatically to the volume of crime as users take cash and possessions from others in a desperate attempt to raise money to pay the dealers. Very often jobs and homes are lost, friendship and family ties are broken. Where children are involved there is a danger of abandonment and neglect. (House of Commons Home Affairs Select Committee, 2002a, p 4)

If prohibition is to mean anything, it must act as a deterrent – a typical utilitarian argument – but when asked to provide evidence the government often struggles to do so, invariably saying that it continues to look into the matter. Assessing the impact of deterrence on any activity is difficult, and almost impossible on a subject as complex as drug taking, but the government continues to restate its commitment to that principle. It believes that prohibition sends the right messages to the majority of young people who do not take drugs, stating that legislation defines what is right and wrong. For example, under the heading 'What works?', the Home Affairs Select Committee (2002b, p 5) stated: 'The law works. The fact that drugs are illegal deters people from misuse and limits experimentation.' It still gave no evidence to support it. In line with Lord Windlesham, and with most prohibitionist arguments, the government in 2002 continued to assert that its policies retained general support, and cited a report of 2000 where 30% of adults questioned by MORI gave illegality as a reason for not taking drugs. The government's position has remained stubbornly clear: 'We reject any call to legalise or decriminalise any currently controlled substances.... Nor does the Government envisage any circumstance in which it would do so' (House of Commons Home Affairs Select Committee, 2002b, p 10). Lord Windelsham again:

> [H]ere, surely, we are faced by a problem of classic proportions. That it is a confusing and difficult question no one would deny. Its dimensions are hard enough to describe; let alone to interpret and understand. But we must make the effort. Were we to stand back and say that the law is powerless in the face of a social phenomenon of this kind we should not only be abandoning a number of gravely sick people, but we should put at risk our interest in the welfare of a substantial part of an entire generation of young people. Professional pushers and other criminals would also be left to their own devices in exploiting, for their own gain, the weaknesses of human nature. (*Hansard*, 14 February 1971)

Prohibition has remained a resolute government position, irrespective of its political hue. The claim that the majority of the population is anti-legalisation is probably correct, but that of course is not a justification for retaining that policy, although it may be an important consideration. The government's further claim that legalisation would wreak untold havoc and suffering remains unshaken, for the prohibitionists continue to point out that legalisation would result in much increased drug use, producing a dramatic increase in attendant health and behavioural problems. And the fear is that once established, they would take years, perhaps generations, to rectify. This may explain why governments fear legalisation, and why they rail against what they see as the irresponsibility of those advocating it. The point is obvious: once the genie is out of the bottle, what then? There is no easy way back, or as Kleiman and Saiger (1990, p 544) put it somewhat sardonically, as Humpty Dumpty demonstrated, not all processes are reversible. Prohibitionists warn against moving into the unknown, which to do so would, they say, become an abdication of government responsibilities. Whether the 'fear of the unknown' is an adequate defence is another matter, but it remains an oft-quoted

14

one. Prohibition stands squarely on the law as protector of the social order, preventing harm to self and others.

Economic liberalism

At one end of the spectrum is prohibition, at the other lies 'economic liberalism'. Here I want to use the term as it applies to that small but eloquent group of economists who define liberalism in terms of a libertarian position arising from a free market. Their central position is that free markets are superior to government-controlled markets in almost every respect, especially in regulating behaviour, and in this case in removing existing illegal markets.

A UK version is offered by Richard Stevenson (1994). In Stevenson's proposal it would no longer be an offence to possess, use or trade in drugs. The distribution and supply should be through the market. Yet Stevenson is not a complete free marketer. He wants sales to be restricted to pharmacists, with the government providing licenses to producers and distributors to market their products. As he makes plain, he is not advocating or encouraging drug use; 'there should be no presumption that an activity is desirable because it is legal' (1994, p 58). Drugs would bear a sternly worded health warning. He says that consideration could be given to legalising some drugs but not others, although he says that such a move should be resisted since it would 'give an incentive to criminals to specialise in the sale of the more dangerous sorts' (1994, p 66). He doubts that a case for prohibition could be made on ethical, social or moral grounds for he says that prohibition implies a faith in the power of governments to protect citizens and suppress illegal markets, which, he adds, experience does not support (1994, p 61).

Stevenson does not make wild and impossible claims, as some do, or give wild predictions about future benefits. To him, legalisation is about assessing the harms done and the benefits gained and, not surprisingly, he concludes that while legalisation may well have some disadvantages, the advantages will outweigh them. So, some users will continue to commit crime, and some criminals will continue to use drugs, but he believes that eventually there will be an overall reduction in drug use. Why? Because many drug users will no longer need to commit crime to finance their habit (1994, p 53). He admits that cannabis use might increase initially, but he hopes that legal drug use would make drug use 'boring'. He insists that the benefits are real; medical benefits would accrue from the replacement of adulterated street drugs with pharmaceutically pure products (1994, p 53). He says the 'principal merit of legalisation is that it would retard the spread of corruption and criminality which threatens the political and legal fabric of whole societies' (1994, pp 54-5). Of course, faced with the fact that there are no legalisation experiments on which to call, his, and all other predictions as to future use have to be considered as speculative, or rather as either optimistic or pessimistic depending on one's point of view. Richard Stevenson is optimistic, even to the point of saying that a fall in prices would be equivalent to an increase in real income for users and their families (1994, p 53).

The theme that runs through this and most proposals from other economic liberals is that the social control of drugs should pass to legitimate businesspeople and away from the organised crime syndicates. 'In illegal markets most of the decisions ... are made by criminals. In legal markets, they are by businessmen within a framework of law' (1994, p 54). Legalisation is not about handing out drugs like giving sweets to schoolchildren, or offering a sentimental view of addiction as if addicts were victims of some great conspiracy, or even a way of removing responsibility. It is about reducing crime and corruption, improving health and reducing cost. It means transferring decisions to the market, making new rules appropriate to a market philosophy, and allowing the market to determine the means of production, supply and distribution. Rules will be there as before, but there will be different rules; this version of liberalism is not anarchy or a free-for-all. It is about offering a different system of control, by the market, not government.

The crucial question is: would the market provide a more coherent and effective control system than the existing one? Its obvious advantage is it would mean that drugs could be purchased openly with a guaranteed level of purity from licensed suppliers, thereby avoiding the trappings of illegality, and removing the powers of the illegal crime syndicates. As such, it is an attractive proposition yet raises a number of questions that these and other legalisers must answer.

Arnold Trebach's version of economic liberalism is founded on his horror that the US would not allow prescriptions of opiates to patients with terminal conditions. He wants to 'deal with virtually all illegal drugs as we now deal with alcohol' (Trebach and Inciardi, 1993, p 80). Trebach is not an economist, and not therefore an 'economic liberal' in the purist sense of the term, but his views have been well stated over time, and his opposition to US prohibition made clear. He is included here as his ideas fit within that general economic framework. Trebach wants to 'repeal national drug prohibition'. How should this be done? 'Just do it. Let the pieces fall as they will' (Trebach and Inciardi, 1993, p 81). This is a cavalier approach, as 'letting the pieces fall' takes no account of where they will fall, who they will fall on, and the likely immediate effect on the various parties. It is a risky, and some would say an irresponsible, strategy. If, as he believes, governments will shy away from such proposals, he offers two options. First, to permit the person to obtain drugs on prescription from a medical practitioner. He rejects this because he says it produces a medical monopoly, and being circumspect, Trebach stands in contrast to those placing their trust in that profession. For example, Trebach fears that as with all monopolies medical decisions will turn out to be unfavourable to its customers, and anyway, in an eagerness to be rid of the paternalism of prohibition there is a danger that it will be swapped for the paternalism of the professional. Not surprisingly, he would prefer the second option, what he calls the non-medical one where, like Stevenson, he would permit an adult to obtain drugs from a licensed seller. Thus, he says, 'the State would be treating adults like adults, or as responsible thinking people who are given choices, and are deemed capable of making them' (Trebach and Inciardi, 1993, p 87). 'Treating adults like adults' is a familiar refrain and a swipe at medical paternalism, which Trebach sees as ingrained within medicine. It is also a swipe at prohibition where paternalism lies deep within the prohibition body politic.

A more forceful version of economic liberalism in the US is found in the writings of Mark Thornton (1998), a free market economist. He offers what he calls 'perfect legalisation' where 'perfect' means elimination of government intervention in the market. More radical than Stevenson, Thornton offers a programme that is extensive, but like Stevenson does not imply that his version offers a complete solution. What Thornton insists is that the government should not discriminate for or against drugs, in the same way that it does not discriminate for or against, say, cornflakes. To the question 'what policies should government choose for drugs?' the only answer, he says, is those policies that extract governments from the drug market. To a free market economist, controls by markets are superior to controls by government. Perfect legalisation offers a free market, where Thornton's version, unlike that of Stevenson, does not include controls over supply and distribution, that is, that sales would be open to all as with cornflakes, and not controlled by anyone including physicians and pharmacists.

Thornton's views are shared by other free marketers such as Milton Friedman and Thomas Szasz (1992) although the latter as a psychiatrist, not an economist, puts a slightly different slant on matters. Nonetheless, Szasz (1996) views drug control as an illegal activity and the consequences irrelevant. That is to say, he is not concerned with the size of the prison population, corrupt officials or the like, only with the merits or defects of the argument. He likens US prohibition and the 'war on drugs' to heresy laws. By that he means prohibition promotes factually incorrect anti-drug propaganda, extols severe punishments and denounces drug dealers in ways that resemble ancient methods of hunting heretics (see Kleiman and Saiger, 1990, p 534; Szasz, 1996).

All free market economists offer the message that the market provides a superior method of supply and distribution than government controls. Their constant theme is that the 'war on drugs' cannot be won, and prohibition makes things worse. Thornton and

Friedman start from a well-established economic theory, which to the free market economist is not obscured by fluffy moralistic statements about pleasure, sin and the purification of society.

Thornton (1998, p 640) says that the 'ideology of Prohibition is an ideology that originated with Puritanism and other heretical religious groups. It is based on the notion that certain objects or goods are the source of sin not the individual sinner.' In practice that means that these goods should be strictly regulated, or better, eliminated entirely if society is to be purified and prepared for the Second Coming.

Thornton notes that this powerful ideology has become increasingly secularised over the years, but the basic features remain intact. He cites and quotes approvingly the comments by Yandle (1983) that prohibition is highly popular among two important groups in the US who have formed a strange coalition, what Yandle calls 'bootleggers and Baptists'. Except that prohibition requires an enforcement policy to operate it, so the coalition expands to 'bootleggers, Baptists and bureaucrats' (Yandle, 1983, p 12). As a result, it becomes much stronger politically. 'Bootleggers, Baptists and bureaucrats' sums things up rather well. The modern version means that 'bootleggers' are those making the money producing and selling the drugs, and the 'bureaucrats' are the lawyers, enforcement officers, judges and so on whose careers depend on catching the 'bootleggers', who are in turn overseen by the 'Baptists', the modern prohibitionists who disapprove of the use of drugs.

Certainly, moral disapproval of drug taking is evident throughout the prohibitionist case. To its critics, prohibition of a self-regarding act amounts to unabridged paternalism. They say that mountaineering is self-regarding and dangerous, so is riding a motorcycle, but governments do not prohibit these. So, why pick on drug taking? The answer to a free marketer like Thornton would be that the moralists like the Baptists eschew any activity that gives unadulterated pleasure without first having exerted an appropriate effort. If pleasure is unearned, it should be banned. The prohibitionist response is that drug taking is more than a self-regarding act, it is also other regarding, having deleterious effects on other members of society, and imposing huge costs on public health facilities. More than that, self-regarding governments have a duty to protect citizens from harmful actions, for example in the use of seat belts, building regulations, and demands that we save for our old age pensions. We do not live in a society where governments slough off responsibility to protect us against harmful actions even if a loss of liberty results; the ancient concept of *parens patriae*, literally the state as father to the people, originally invoked for Chancery Lunatics and Wards of Court, but applied in many areas of the welfare state, provides strong and persistent precedents that cannot be ignored.

Thornton is an ardent free marketer; not everyone goes that far. Other economists such as Stevenson appear to baulk at this extreme position, modifying and thereby placing limitations on the free market philosophy. They want to control and limit the consumption of goods (drugs) via a network of government interventions. This is modified prohibition, and to Thornton a shoddy compromise, which, because it does not eliminate the black market, actually makes the problem worse. Perfect legalisation, in contrast, Thornton says, does eliminate the black market, alongside prohibition-related crime and corruption.

There is something appealing about Thornton's approach. Its direct simplicity is attractive – 'simplicity' in the sense of being straightforward and uncomplicated. His critique of reformist measures such as harm reduction is instructive because he sees them as promoting a lull in the cycle of failed prohibitionist policies. Changing to a modified form of prohibition such as introducing harm reduction policies might reduce some of the social costs but, he says, cannot and will not eliminate the black market, the crime or corruption associated with prohibition (Thornton, 1998, pp 642, 644). Harm reduction, says Thornton (1998, p 640), 'calls for a shifting of resources to reduce the costs of prohibition'. It will mean that some of the direct effects of prohibition will be reduced, but other forms of government intervention such as demand reduction and drug substitution policies will be increased. Harm reduction 'does reduce the social cost of prohibition in the short run, but the policy shifting will be shown to be crucial for the long term stability of the prohibitionist regime because it does not address the underlying problems' (1998, p 640).

This, coupled with the belief that interventionist policies always make matters worse, offers a proposal that is intrinsically appealing. There is something about it which suggests that we might be able to break the shackles we have imposed on ourselves, and on the restrictions on our thinking. The absence of government controls and the triumph of the consumer as king in a free market offer an attractive alternative. So too does Thornton's dislike and distrust of so-called 'drug experts' who, he says, have little knowledge of market analysis, less than average experience in real-world markets and no experience in political accountability. Yet attractive though Thornton's position may be, what stops me from accepting it? Timidity perhaps? Certainly, his views on the purchase of drugs by all, including juveniles, are worrying, but more because there is a fear that his proposals might lead to a massive and wholesale increase in drug use and addiction. He would see that as the utilitarian coming to the fore, or the timid prohibitionist coming to the surface, but I see him as offering a potentially dangerous programme, which could, in the name of economic theory, go sadly wrong. Stevenson (1994, p 62) says 'the legal use of drugs would make drug use boring. Indeed there are good reasons to suppose that harm would be reduced', while Friedman (Friedman and Szasz, 1992) says that individuals should be the guardian of their own behaviour. Perhaps they should, but what if drug use does not become boring, and what happens to those who cannot be the guardian of their behaviour? Who cares for them?

Legal moralists

Thus far I have concentrated on free market economists and avoided political considerations, yet the contribution of organisations such as Liberty and of those who assert the right to use drugs (Husak, 1992) cannot be ignored. Incidentally, the term 'legal moralist' is inadequate for a number of reasons, but it is difficult to find another more suitable one. As used here it refers to those who regard the intrusion of the law as a violation of the fundamental rights to use recreational drugs, and as such means an unjustified intrusion of the state in the personal lives of its citizens. Legal moralists are not advocating the use of drugs; they simply assert that an individual has the right to use them if they want to.

Liberty considers that, as part of a free democratic society, individuals should be able to make and carry out informed decisions as to their conduct, and be free of state interference, unless there are pressing reasons otherwise. Liberty is of the view that the decision by an individual to take drugs does not constitute such a pressing reason, and as such comes within the ambit of personal autonomy and private life. It quotes approvingly John Stuart Mill's dictum that the state has no right to intervene to prevent individuals from harming themselves, if no harm is thereby done to the rest of society. 'Over himself, over his own body and mind, the individual is sovereign' (Mill, 1948, p 4). It concludes that 'Such fundamental rights are recognised by government, both in allowing individuals to partake of certain dangerous activities, for example drinking, extreme sports, and also in international treaties' (Liberty, 2001).

Liberty's submission to the Home Affairs Select Committee laid out the philosophical reasons for this being desirable:

> [A]s part of a free, democratic society individuals should be able to make and carry out informed decisions as to their conduct, free of state interference, or in particular the criminal law, unless there are pressing social reasons otherwise. Liberty is of the view that the decision by an individual to take drugs is such a decision and comes within the ambit of personal autonomy and private life. (Liberty, 2001, para 3)

It further stated:

—

22

> In a society that respects fundamental freedoms of the individual, and in particular the right to individual autonomy and choice, general restrictions and criminalisation of taking of drugs cannot be justified. (Liberty, 2001, para 7)

Liberty is not a full-scale legaliser of the order of Thornton, as it accepts the need for some regulation and control over selected groups of users:

> We would not argue for complete deregulation of all drugs. We accept that there are circumstances which will require regulations and in some cases criminalisation of aspects of supply and consumption of drugs. These would for example be the supply of drugs to minors or those suffering from certain forms of mental illness. (Liberty, 2001, para 8)

This, of course, leads to complications, as will be highlighted in subsequent chapters, but Liberty concludes with a return to a John Stuart Mill type argument that such fundamental rights and freedoms are recognised by government in allowing individuals to take part in dangerous activities, for example drinking and extreme sports (Liberty, 2001).

Liberty would find agreement with other legal moralists such as Husak (1992) who have similar objections to prohibition. They both start from a different premise to the economists, and of course the route to their conclusions differ widely, yet all agree that prohibition creates more evils than it prevents. The legal moralists, at least those of the Husak persuasion, begin with the question concerning the best principled reasons for denying that adults have a moral right to use any or all recreational drugs (Husak, 1992, p 5). The right to use a recreational substance may appear trivial, except that in doing so the full force of the criminal law is brought down on the users, resulting in some cases in lengthy prison sentences. This leads Husak (1992, p 3) to ask two related questions: does the state have the legitimate authority to punish adults who use drugs recreationally, and what

---

properties must a hypothetical drug possess before the state has that authority to prohibit it?

This is not a utilitarian argument. To Husak, utilitarian solutions are about whether some clever policy maker is able to provide an answer to this or that social problem. It matters little to Husak whether the 'war on drugs' (which he says is a misnomer anyway – it is a 'war on drug users') or some such policy involving prohibition might proceed to a victory, although the legal moralist like anyone else would view this as welcome. It is about something more fundamental, about the citizen's relationship to the state, the powers of the state and the rights of citizens. That of course opens up central questions in political theory about the nature of rights, including questions of paternalism, and autonomy. All well beyond the scope here, but matters that should not be ignored.

It is not possible to summarise the complexities of Husak's arguments except to say that his conclusions are similar to those who seek justification of the use of the criminal law in the extent and nature of serious harms to others. Every genuinely harmful act justifiably violates rights, but if, as Husak believes, those violations occur only in limited circumstances, as he claims is the case with drug abuse, then prohibition turns out to be an unjustified exercise of state power over individual liberty (1992, p 166). In Husak's terms, these limited circumstances often turn out to produce nothing more than irresponsible behaviour such as inattentive parents, bad neighbours, poor students and unreliable employees, hardly a justification for criminal legislation, although such behaviour may be undesirable. These are primarily harms to oneself, but even then most users do not come to harm. For those who do, this is unfortunate but not a matter for the criminal law; the criminal law is rarely used or justified on the grounds of harms caused to oneself. And while legalisation might lead to an increase in use then which rights are being violated if someone decides to use drugs when they did not use them before? Husak's conclusion is that the arguments in favour of conceding that adults have a moral right to use drugs recreationally are more persuasive than those in favour of prohibition.

I shall refer again to criminal legislation based on the serious harm principle in the final chapter; here I want to set out what Husak sees as the properties that a drug should have in order that the state could justifiably prohibit it. He believes the drug should have the following:

- First, it must increase the likelihood that users will cause a commensurate harm that should be considered a criminal offence caused directly or deliberately.
- Second, the harm caused by use must be substantial.
- Third, the use of the drug must be sufficiently proximate to the consummated harm, that is, it must be more than a necessary condition but a sufficient condition of use.
- Finally, the drug must actually cause a significant percentage of users to commit the commensurate offence. That means that 'research would have to establish that the tendency to violate the rights of others did not predate the consumption of the drug and that no common cause could explain both the propensity to harm others as well as the use of the drug' (Husak, 1992, p 208).

The criteria are stringent, and clearly most of the drugs currently controlled would fail to meet the test. Some would; crack/cocaine would pass, so too would 'ice' (a form of methamphetamine), heroin might, but the hallucinogens such as cannabis and LSD would surely not. How does this fit with current government policy? The House of Commons Home Affairs Select Committee (2002a, para 148) would agree about crack/cocaine:

> Where crack is concerned we see no prospect for compromise. We note that few of our witnesses argued outright for legalisation. We leave it to those who do argue for general legalisation to explain how this could be justified given that, unlike other illegal drugs, crack triggers violent and unpredictable behaviour.

The British government agrees: 'We hold the view that all drugs are harmful, that crack/cocaine is one of the most destructive.' It then added 'and that no illicit drug should be decriminalised or legalised' (Home Affairs Select Committee, 2002b, p 17). Its attitude to this and other controlled drugs confirms Husak's darkest suspicions, that there is no interest in legislative reform. Husak (1992, p 7) suspects, rightly, that the 'current political climate is unfavourable to the decriminalisation of any recreational drugs'.

Irrespective of the merits of the arguments, the ideological preferences of the legal moralists are at odds with those shaping current policy. The freedoms they pronounce are no longer seen with the same clarity or purpose as hitherto, or if they are then only by a small minority. The majority have different preferences, leaving Liberty and others similarly placed, almost as if they were on the wrong side of history. Nowadays we want solutions, actions not freedoms, controls rather than individual decisions. We put up with government intrusions unheard of by and unacceptable to our Victorian forebears and to subscribers of John Stuart Mill's version of liberty. CCTV cameras, seat belts and so on are all justified in the name of protection, with positive freedoms being the accepted modes of living. Liberty and the likes of Husak become lone voices in an otherwise interventionist world, and with little chance of their message being accepted, whether by governments or by the rest of us. Husak's cry goes unheeded, as does that of Liberty.

Concerned as we are with solutions, then how far along that road are we to go before those solutions begin to impinge on our freedoms? In 1997, John Grieve, then a commander in the Metropolitan Police, and with considerable experience of the drug problem in London, said that if that problem continued to advance then we were going to be faced with some very frightening options. Either there had to be a massive reduction in civil rights or some radical solutions had to be found. He questioned whether a criminal justice system could solve this particular problem (Channel 4 television, 1997). He said this faced with mounting criticisms of police practice, knowing too that the amounts of drugs seized appeared to have little impact on the size of the problem. He was also aware that a number of High Court decisions had placed strains on an already overstretched police force, producing a further disabling effect, especially over the use of informants on which the police place great reliance.[1] John Grieve's question was if the police are to remain a viable force, able to keep pace with the extent of illegal drug activity, then one option is to give them more powers, but more powers means fewer rights for the rest of us.

The dilemma is real: interventionist solutions or liberty? The choice may turn out to be less stark. More likely there will be a steady drip of control, leading to a slow erosion of liberty. It would begin with an extension of the control system, such as an increase in CCTV cameras, then new provisions of 'stop and search', followed by a relaxation in the rules of evidence, and so on and so on. All would be justified as reducing crime. Liberty will protest, but few will take notice. The problems will be presented as too great and too immediate to worry about freedoms.

Fortunately, legal moralists raise questions others prefer to ignore. Freedom may not be an absolute value but it is worth preserving and once lost difficult to regain. The legal moralists expose the weakness of those eager to solve problems where intervention becomes a worthy option, and where the assumption is sustained that all social problems can be solved if only the right solutions can be identified. But they may not, and even if they were, the result may be a further loss of liberty. Nowhere is this more apparent than the way we continue to increase the numbers of controlled substances, all called 'harmful' yet rarely with any clear definition of the nature or extent of harm. Losing our rights to take certain drugs may not be important in the grand scheme of things yet each loss of liberty also weakens the quality of our lives.

Note

[1] Two High Court cases are relevant. Both involve the use of informants, and both require that the names of the informants be disclosed. These cases have implications for police practice, for if they can no longer

guarantee the informants anonymity, they will be reluctant to provide information. In *R v Turner* (1994), a request to disclose the identity of the informant was wrongly turned down as the informant's identity was relevant to the defence case. The Court of Appeal ruled that the identity should have been disclosed. In the other case – *R v Taylor* (1994) – the Court ruled that a defendant in a criminal trial has a fundamental right to see and know the identity of their accusers, including witnesses for the prosecution. The Court said that this right should only be denied in rare and exceptional circumstances, and that a balance must be struck between the needs of the prosecution witnesses and the fairness of the trial.

3

Harm reduction, medicalisation and decriminalisation

In this chapter I want to look at harm reduction, medicalisation and decriminalisation, the three reformative, rather than radical features of the debate. These fit more easily into those proposals that soften or mitigate the impact of prohibition. They are less about removing controls, more often about changing direction.

Harm reduction

The Canadian Centre on Substance Abuse Working Group (1996) outlines five principles of harm reduction, which it says allow drug use to be acknowledged, but not judged, with action to be supportive, not punitive. These principles are:

- *pragmatism* – being realistic and recognising that drug taking carries risk and accepting that abstinence is not necessarily attainable or desirable;
- *humanistic values*, which means respect for the worth and dignity of all persons including drug users;
- *reducing the negative consequences of drug use*, which may not necessarily be promoted by focusing on decreasing or eliminating use;
- *examining the costs and benefits of drug use* in order to arrive at that balance between promoting individual and common good (supervised injection facilities are an example of such a balance);
- *focusing on and giving priority to the goals listed above*, using democratic values of collaboration and participation with those who are marginalised in society.

The International Harm Reduction Association, which began in 1996, is more specific. It says that harm reduction refers to policies and programmes that attempt primarily to reduce the adverse health, social and economic consequences of mood-altering substances to individual drug users, their families and their communities (International Harm Reduction Association, 1996, 2008).

Taken together, these principles provide an adequate summary of the main features of harm reduction programmes. Most are not contentious, and anyway aimed at such a high level of generality as to be of little direct practical value. Contained within them are suggestions that harm reduction is not concerned with abstinence, nor is there much sympathy with prohibition. Harm reduction involves a recognition that drug abuse is here to stay, at least in the foreseeable future; accordingly, plans must be made to mitigate its evils rather than expect quick-fire solutions. That presumably is also what is meant by 'pragmatism', which in this context leads its critics to refer to what they call a 'poverty of ambition', and a too-ready acceptance of the existing state of affairs. The International Association makes no distinction between harm to the user and harm to the community. This is puzzling for it presumably means that harm to self is of the same order as harm to others – a difficult position to sustain in the light of contemporary criminal sanctions.

The criminal law has consistently justified penalties involving harm to others as being more blameworthy than harm to self. In spite of these inconsistencies, Ethan Nadelmann (1999a) sees harm reduction as offering a rational approach to policy. He wants us to imagine a policy that starts by acknowledging that drugs are here to stay, and that we have no choice but to live with them. The aim then is to see that they cause the least possible harm. Imagine too, he says, a policy that focuses on reducing the crime and misery caused by drug abuse and prohibitionist policies. And imagine a drug policy based not on fear, prejudice and ignorance, but rather on common sense, science, public health concerns and human rights. That policy, says Nadelmann, is harm reduction (Nadelmann, 1999a, p 158). Incidentally, one gets the impression that Nadelmann is talking to a US audience, which has hitherto been slow to embrace harm reduction programmes.

Harm reduction developed in the UK at a timely moment, coinciding with and receiving additional impetus during the HIV/AIDS crisis in the 1980s when there were fears that HIV/AIDS was being spread by drug users sharing dirty needles and other non-sterile injecting practices (ACMD, 1988). The fear was realistic and the emphasis on harm reduction appropriate. Harm reduction has expanded exponentially since then, and its international reach is there for all to see. It can count among its supporters the UN General Assembly, which on 2 June 2001 unanimously declared the importance of harm reduction (UN General Assembly Declaration of Commitment Special Session on HIV/AIDS), linking it to its Declaration on HIV/AIDS (UN General Assembly, 2006, pp 1-6). It has received support from numerous academics and commentators on drug policy. Peter Reuter (1992) approvingly calls supporters of harm reduction 'owls', that is, of a group lying midway between 'hawks' and 'doves', and Ethan Nadlemann (1999a, p 162) rails against the US government, believing that as a conservative estimate 10,000 people have been infected with HIV in the US as a result of its failure to institute harm reduction programmes. He gives harm reduction unequivocal support, saying that drug control programmes should focus on reducing drug-related crime, disease and death, not on the number of casual users, adding that stopping the spread of HIV by making sterile needles and methadone available must be the first priority (1999a, p 172). And to further demonstrate its global reach, the International Harm Reduction Association (2008, p 119) claims that increasingly UN human rights monitors have begun to interpret the provisions of harm reduction interventions as necessary for states to be compliant with the right to health.

In its clearest form, harm reduction is about finding ways to reduce the harm of drug use, while emphasising the importance of a public health model for reducing risks and consequences. Its philosophical foundation is Benthamite utilitarianism, although never acknowledged; Bentham urged the importance of deterrence and the value of reducing levels of unhappiness by selected policies. He saw it as an advance if an offender could be persuaded to commit less serious offences than hitherto. So too with harm reduction: better to encourage users to inject with sterile needles, or take cannabis rather than cocaine.

There is little doubt that harm reduction has been a dominant force in contemporary drug policies, perhaps more so in the UK than elsewhere. It has an obvious appeal best summarised by Ethan Nadelmann's (quoted in Husak, 1998, p 35) question 'Who in their right minds could oppose the notion of reducing harm?' Except that when one looks more closely, things become less clear. For example, the International Harm Reduction Association (1996, p 1) says that there are two main pillars that guide harm reduction – 'a pragmatic public health approach, and the other based on human rights' – which it claims are aimed at avoiding value-laden terms such as 'drug abuse' and 'drug addict'. It is not clear what this means or which aspects of public health are to be emphasised. Clearly, there is little or no dispute that the prevention of HIV/AIDS should be dominant but which others? Is the provision of sterile needles to reduce the impact of hepatitis C to be considered more important than attempts to decrease the numbers who inject? Or are crime reduction programmes more important than offering condoms to prostitutes? Or is prescribing methadone more important than discouraging new users? If so, might promoting the former increase the latter? Or put another way, assume two available policies, and suppose Policy A produces less harm to users than policy B, then presumably Policy A would be preferred. But what happens if Policy A turns out to be harmful to non-users. Which then is to be preferred? For are harms to users to be given the same status as harms to non-users? To complicate matters further, are harms to be offset against benefits, for once 'benefits' are introduced the equation becomes even more complicated? The problem then changes into how to identify benefits and how to balance them against harms or costs (Husak, 1998, pp 35-6).

—

Given the wide remit and comprehensive approach, splinter groups have inevitably developed. For example, growing out of the mainstream movement has been harm minimisation, which is more comprehensive. It includes demand reduction, aimed at discouraging new users but encouraging existing users towards abstinence. Harm reduction also includes supply control, which means regulating the control of drugs whether through law enforcement or legislation. Although harm minimisation has received less formal attention, many harm reduction programmes should more correctly be called harm minimisation. For example, the Australian government's policy in relation to alcohol and other drugs these past 20 years has been a typical harm minimisation programme. Also, David Blakey (BBC Radio 4, 11 September 2008), an ex-chief constable, suggested a programme aimed at reducing harm but which is classical harm minimisation. It includes reducing availability, reducing demand through deterrence, encouraging users into treatment and adopting traditional harm reduction practices, for example needle exchange schemes; but also prosecuting dealers and breaking up drug markets. Or, again, some harm reductionists have been willing to trade increases in drug use for decreases in harm (Reuter and MacCoun, 1996). 'Harm', it seems, can be interpreted widely. Different again is 'gradualism', which includes traditional harm reduction policies but urges its users towards abstinence, if and when windows of opportunity occur. These splinter groups illustrate tensions within the movement where supporters of harm minimisation and gradualism view traditional harm reduction as rooted in what they call 'low expectations'.

Harm reduction is not without its critics. Some see it as nothing more than a platform, or an approach to a series of policy options, rather than a policy in its own right. Might not Ethan Nadelmann's question of 'who in their right minds oppose the notion of reducing harm' be applied to any social problem? Overeating? The education system? The National Health Service (NHS) even? (Husak, 1998, p 48). Others seek answers to the question of whether harm reduction is concerned with minimising harm or maximising benefits. For if

—

the former then harm reduction should concentrate on users, but if the latter then on non-users, offering an entirely different emphasis. Finally, there are critics concerned with the moral implications of harm reduction, matters that are denied by its supporters who claim that harm reduction avoids all value-laden terms, a curious position given its terminology. 'Harm' is a moral term, for to ask what is a harm is to ask what makes that harmful. Moreover, harm reduction is concerned with 'rights'. Determining and protecting rights are moral enterprises – which incidentally one would have thought would be to the credit of harm reductionists, rather than be denied.

Sadly, harm reduction has become entwined with all sorts of political positions, and as its critics tirelessly point out, and with some truth, it has often become an apology for the drug culture, or as a cloak for a less strident form of legalisation. On the face of it, harm reduction should assume a central position somewhere between the prohibitionists and the radicals, but is often presented as more sympathetic to the latter. One critic calls it 'a hijacked concept that has become a euphemism for legalisation. It's a cover story for people who would lower the barriers to drug use' (McCaffrey, quoted in Kleber and Inciardi, 2005, p 1384). If it has, and I think it has, its position is weakened. Its strength has always been to acknowledge drug use as a chronic condition, yet stress the need to reduce detrimental effects, while reigning in overzealous legislators, or providing facilities to reduce unwelcome side-effects, such as improving health, and reducing crime alongside other deleterious social consequences; for example, by the introduction of needle exchange schemes to reduce the risk of users passing on HIV/AIDS by sharing injection equipment. If harm reduction is to achieve its potential, it needs to promote a clear statement about future direction; is it within a prohibitionist framework, or a step towards legalisation? Muddying the waters helps no one.

Harm reduction policies and programmes are effective when they concentrate on needle exchange schemes, supervise injection facilities, help users avoid overdoses, as well as prevent and reduce multiple harms including a reduction in the risk of HIV, hepatitis

C, overdoses, soft tissue infections and respiratory problems. This in spite of the desperate backgrounds of so many users. 'Histories of childhood abuse, economic and social disadvantage, the presence of mental illness, lack of social support and family dysfunction are more likely among those who are street involved' (Pauly, 2008). Not all harm reduction programmes have been successful. Mike Ashton (2003) reports on studies in Vancouver where there was limited evidence for the reduction in risks from needle exchange as one in five of local injectors shared needles even when they had no problems getting fresh supplies. Harm reduction programmes can of course operate alongside or within prohibition; there is no necessary conflict between them, although conflict will occur with zero tolerance type policies, which involve harassing and prosecuting all forms of drug taking. These leave harm reduction with little or no room to manoeuvre.[1]

A main platform of harm reduction has been methadone maintenance, which can also operate within and alongside prohibition. Methadone maintenance was introduced by Dole and Nyswander in 1965 and is claimed to restrict the highs and lows of heroin use, thereby helping control the addict's behaviour. Its main function is to prevent the emergence of opiate withdrawal and the craving that occurs when heroin blood levels fall below a certain point. Many claims are made for its effectiveness (Farrell et al, 1994; Brewer, 2004; Pauly, 2008). The National Treatment Agency (NTA) published a briefing on the effectiveness of prescribed medication for drug misusers, and concluded that oral methadone has the best evidence base, and therefore should be available in every area of the country (NTA, 2003a). This support from the NTA, a government-funded initiative, gave a resounding vote of confidence to a programme that was becoming increasingly criticised. For at about this time the critics were beginning to circle. Was methadone maintenance nothing more than a way of controlling the white working class? And how often did those on methadone maintenance kick the habit? Was not methadone simply another addictive drug, and if so how was this construed as treatment?

Not only were the critics beginning to circle but their arrows were beginning to hit their targets. 'Once on methadone they may be trapped in limbo for years' was how Melanie Reid, writing in *The Times* (3 October 2008), described the addict's plight. 'Say no, no, no, to the rehab industry.' She further described methadone maintenance as 'creating a pharmaceutical holding pen' that keeps addicts addicted. This is not what methadone maintenance was supposed to be about. Colin Brewer (2004, p 101), a supporter of methadone maintenance, talks of 'maturing out', which means that a significant number of opiate-dependent persons will, he expects, spontaneously discontinue opiate use when they reach a certain age, usually their late twenties or early thirties. Whether this is enough to satisfy critics is difficult to say. Methadone maintenance is increasingly seen as being on the dark side of harm reduction, its supporters constantly avoiding tricky questions about abstinence and creating the suspicion that it is more about controlling users than providing treatment. That is not a wholesome outcome.

In a curious irony, harm reductionists' most ardent critics began to gather momentum at about the same time that Gerry Stimson was making his most triumphant comments to the International Harm Reduction Association (IHRA, 2008) He claimed: 'In many ways the scientific debate has been won, and only ideological and moralistic criticisms remain' (IHRA, 2008, p 119). These claims were premature. At the time he was claiming victory, the so-called 'new abstentionists' arrived:

> Around bonfire night (5th November) 2007 a rocket shook the peak of England's drug treatment structure – some asked how many patients ended up drug free. Clothesless as the fabled Emperor, '3%' came the reply.... The new abstentionists were on the march and the statistics seemed to be on their side. (Ashton, 2007, p 1)

Indeed they were. The '3%' arose as a result of a question to the chief executive officer of the National Treatment Agency by the BBC as to how many drug users who had received treatment were abstinent. The reply was that in England at the end of 2006/07 just 3% were recorded as having completed treatment and were drug free. That 3% figure occurred again, this time in Scotland, when Professor Neil McKeganey reported that only 3% of methadone patients were reported clean within three years of being in treatment. The shibboleth of harm reduction began to be challenged, this time not on moral but on empirical grounds.

Three per cent was seen as a paltry figure when set against the enormous costs of harm reduction programmes; methadone maintenance costs about £1,000 per patient per annum for the drugs alone. The abstentionists rightly asked about the other 97%. Were they still addicted? Was harm reduction extending their addiction? Did not most users on methadone wish to be drug free – it was difficult to believe that most of the 97% saw addiction as their long-term goal. Ethan Nadelmann's question began to seem increasingly hollow. 'Who in their right minds could support a programme with so few results?' became a pressing alternative. The persistent refusal to entertain abstinence or promote any form of abstinence-based treatment was coming home to roost. In Scotland, the 3% figure prompted a dramatic policy U-turn, senior government figures being convinced that addicts should be pressured to get themselves clean (Ashton, 2007, p 3). 'The Scottish Executive has recently faced up to the obvious and recognised what has long stared it in the face that doling out methadone is not the answer' (Dalrymple, *The Times*, 30 May 2008, p 21).

Hawks and Lenton (1995) offer a useful summary of the achievements of harm reduction, saying that overall studies suggest that methadone maintenance reduces heroin use, injection-related risks and premature mortality among opioid users. It is far more effective when doses over 50mg are employed and when the treatment is not aimed at abstinence (1995, p 298). It reduces or eliminates cravings and avoids the symptoms of opioid withdrawal, but its critics say that it merely substitutes one addiction for another. Not all harm reduction strategies are successful but some are, and if there has to be a choice between preventing HIV/AIDS and in doing so increasing drug abuse then there is no contest. Credit must be given to the manner in which harm reduction strategies have helped stave off the spread of HIV, but not all matters are so clear cut, and not all harms so extreme.

Set against any achievements are nagging questions about what harm reduction – as exemplified by methadone maintenance – is trying to do. Its opposition to abstinence, or perhaps more correctly its indifference to abstinence, has angered many. The Conservative Party, for example, sees harm reduction strategies as perpetuating addiction, with treatments involving abstinence being marginalised (Gyngell, 2007). (Opposition to US-style drug courts being introduced in the UK, which involve strict abstinence programmes, is an obvious example.) Melanie Reid (2008) puts the point more forcibly: she says that the Conservatives would like to steer their policy towards abstinence, 'But then so did Tony Blair and Gordon Brown when they came to office only to be beaten down by the powerful methadone lobby'. In this she has a point; the methadone lobby, although not a formal grouping, is powerful and influential, and does not easily accept criticism or opposition. Yet harm reduction must meet the criticism that it opposes abstinence and creates a perception that drug use can be undertaken safely.

How to assess harm reduction within the scheme of things? Critics such as the legal moralists see the long-term effects of harm reduction as promoting prohibition, for harm reduction merely props up prohibitionist regimes. Harm reduction policies are traditionally embedded in policies that involve government control and the regulation of drugs. Harm reduction has no interest in the debate about the right to use drugs, or the right to privacy, which legal moralists say is violated by prohibition. Nor does harm reduction fit easily with economic liberty. Thornton (1998) says that harm reduction simply shifts resources to reduce the cost of prohibition onto drug users and taxpayers. That means that while the direct cost of prohibition is reduced, other forms of government interventions are increased. The long-term effect of harm reduction is to sustain prohibition, for it becomes a trade-off between the costs of prohibition and the costs of drug abuse (1998, p 644). Nor does it address the problem of supply. What it does, and what it can do effectively, is soften the harms created by prohibition. Claims to do more are inappropriate and out of place.

Medicalisation

If harm reduction has been criticised, medicalisation remains firmly popular, perhaps due to the way it has been marketed, and its close affinity to harm reduction, albeit with the sharp edges removed. As used here, medicalisation means legally prescribing drugs to users, the user presumably having been assessed by a member of the medical profession, who also decides on the dosage and the drug to be prescribed.

Those favouring medicalisation say that the prescribing of drugs to addicts has a number of advantages, one of which is that prescribed drugs do not contain dangerous impurities. In an obvious sense, this must be so. In a small study we carried out on the pharmacological content of ecstasy tablets (Bean, 1984), purchased from illegal markets, we found that they contained a variety of substances, mostly caffeine, but also rat poison alongside various other equally unpleasant substances. The price of the drugs and the venue where they were purchased had no relationship to their quality. Expensive drugs purchased in clubs and pubs had the same defects as those purchased in the street. Worse than that, the strength of the dose varied, again unrelated to price. Quality control did not exist, to the danger and detriment to the user.

The second major advantage claimed by medicalisers is that the status of the user shifts from offender to patient. This, it is said, helps change the nature, character and disposition of drug use. The Rolleston Committee in 1926 stated that heroin and morphine addicts should be treated as sick people, and in need of medical treatment, which may include the prescribing of heroin (Ministry of Health, 1926). The so-called British system from the 1920s did just that, rather less energetically after the late 1970s, but the basis remains

—

39

– about 500 heroin addicts are still legally prescribed heroin, and this is in addition to the unknown numbers being prescribed other drugs including methadone. In the 1960s, at the height of the medicalisation era, cocaine was also prescribed (as cocaine hydrochloride), to be taken in its injectable form alongside heroin. Crack, the modern variant, is a recent phenomenon, and as far as I know has never been prescribed. However, to what extent those who were prescribed heroin in the 1960s were regarded as 'patients' rather than 'addicts', or whether they adopted the sick role and the prescribing doctor adopted the typical medical role, is difficult to say. It is unlikely that prescribing heroin changed their deviant identity, whether of their self-perception, or of others including the prescribers.

This of course raises the oft-neglected question about the role of the medical profession in such procedures, obviously a prerequisite for medicalisation. Bakalar and Grinspoon (1984, p 124) show how much we rely on the medical profession to supply the ritual context in which drug technology is made safe and acceptable: 'A medical definition provides a stay against confusion.' This means that medicine decides the safety of a drug, who should receive it, who should handle it, how much to take and what its regulatory body – the General Medical Council (GMC) – will do if those rules are violated. The profession, including the GMC and the British Medical Association, will have a major voice in all medicalisation proposals, determining how the drugs are to be taken (injected or otherwise), whether on private or NHS prescriptions and who will be the prescribers and the prescribed. It may even decide whether to invoice users who require medical treatment (for example as a result of an overdose) in the same way that insurance companies of patients in road traffic accidents are invoiced for treatment in hospital.

The point is a simple one, but no less powerful for that; the medicalisation argument relies on the cooperation and goodwill of the medical profession. That leads to two obvious questions: what is in it for the profession, and what happens if the profession chooses not to cooperate? The answer to the first is simple: not a great deal it seems. Drug users as patients are not to every physician's liking, they are often disruptive and difficult to handle. Many so-called 'junkie doctors' have come to grief whether through overprescribing, injudicious treatment or impropriety with patients. Too few physicians want to be involved in drug treatment programmes. If the answer to the second is that the profession as a whole does not wish to cooperate, that would be the end of medicalisation. We haven't reached that stage yet, but it is conceivable that the profession might, in the future, refuse to prescribe. After all, maintenance prescribing is not treatment, more akin to the management of chronic diseases such as diabetes (DH, 2003; NTA, 2003b).

Medicalisation, like harm reduction, is multifaceted. For some, it means offering addicts prescription drugs, the amounts based on the nature of their addiction. For others, it means providing users with the drug of choice on demand. Robert Karel (1991), a medicaliser in the US, offers a more expansive approach with a cumbersome administrative structure attached. As a medicaliser he wants the physician to be able to prescribe various psychoactive drugs based on the professional judgement of the physician and the clinical (drug) needs of the patient (1991, p 88). He then adds a set of complex bureaucratic demands. For example, not all drugs would be instantly prescribed. Cocaine would only be available in small quantities, in packets of 1g at a time, and then only one packet every 48 to 72 hours. Purchase would be through a bank teller system. For psychedelic drugs such as peyote and LSD, the provisions would also be conditional, only available where the user could demonstrate knowledge of their effects through a written examination. Heroin would be prescribed, and the user encouraged but not forced to abstain. PCP would not be available at all, producing of course, or continuing with, the same black market that Karel wishes to remove. Nonetheless, he hopes that 'With law enforcement freed from the pursuit of other drugs it will be possible to focus on drugs such as PCP', presumably to reduce their use (Karel, 1991, p 87).

Karel's proposal links law enforcement to medicalisation, but if introduced would produce endless complications for all concerned, including the users themselves. Yet Karel recognises the need to fit drugs into appropriate categories, and avoid a one-fits-all situation. In doing so, paradoxically, he illustrates some of the inherent complexities of such a programme. A further aim has been to preserve the twin pillars of medicalisation, that is, improving the quality of the lives of users through medical intervention, and relieving them of the fear of law enforcement. He believes that his proposal will restore the right of physicians to prescribe drugs as they see fit, a right taken away in the US by the 1913 Harrison Act. Unfortunately for Karel, this is not appreciated or approved by everyone. Levine (1993) thinks that some (US) physicians might accept medicalisation but only where the user recognises his dependency as undesirable and tries to mitigate against its destructive effects. The patient must accept the sick role (1993, p 334). British physicians, coming from a different tradition, might be more agreeable. One could see how the profession in Britain might be attracted to such a programme with its emphasis on prevention. Equally, one could see how it might not. Recreational drug prescribing involves physicians responding to the non-medical desires of users (1993, p 327). That is not treatment. Moreover, it is by no means certain that prescribing psychoactive substances such as heroin (or cocaine) encourages users to be disease free. It did not in the 1960s as a tour around the public lavatories of Piccadilly Circus would testify, and it may not do so again.

Stripped of its dross, medicalisation often boils down to another pro-public health and anti-crime crusade (Schmoke, 1990). A journalist, Mary Ann Seighart, writing in *The Times* (14 December 2006), believes that the advantages of medicalisation are clear: 'all this crime and suffering could be wiped out were drugs to be free on prescription.... Hundreds of thousands could be treated as patients rather than criminals.' Is this realistic or just plain longing? After all, why should 'all this crime and suffering' suddenly disappear as a result of drugs being on prescription? Clearly, some individuals needlessly suffer as a result of injecting impure drugs and that could be reduced by government controls. But as shown in the 1960s, careful use rarely occurred in spite of drugs being available on prescription, with death rates high, and infection rampant. In spite of the availability of sterile

42

needles, users did not always use them. Prescribing, at least in the generous way it was often done then, did little to stop the spread of addiction; rather, it did much to encourage it. For the problem remains: how much to prescribe? No one, medical practitioner or otherwise, is able to gauge the amount an addict requires, or wants, except after prolonged observation. Too little and the user buys the drugs elsewhere, too much and the surplus (spillage) is sold. Requiring the user to take their drugs under supervision is hardly appealing, whether to doctor or to patient.

The journalist quoted above cited the Transform Drug Policy Foundation, an active campaigning organisation and a supporter of medicalisation. Transform wants a system that it calls 'legally regulated markets'. Under this the government would regulate and control the production, supply and use of currently illegal drugs (Transform, 2006). Transform is keen to distance itself from any suggestion that it is advocating a 'drugs free for all' strategy, as some critics have suggested. Nor does it want regulated drug markets to be confused with a free market model as espoused by libertarians and free marketers. It wants to replace prohibition with a system of control through the medical and pharmaceutical professions, where users will receive supplies or take their drugs within a state-regulated system. The advantage, it says, is that the production, sale and distribution of the drug of choice will effectively be on demand, which will put it out of the control of criminal organisations.

What is this regulated drug market? It is certainly not harm reduction. While Transform is happy to see harm reduction principles inform current policy, it does not see it as a rational and sustainable policy. In fact it sees it as a contradiction where public health necessities collide with prohibition, or in Transform's terms collide with dogmatic enforcement. Moreover, while harm reduction can be useful for dealing with some of the negative effects of illegal drug misuse, Transform correctly states that it has no impact on harms associated with illegal production and supply (Transform, 2006, p 12). Perhaps it was never intended to do so, but Transform is not alone in citing this weakness. Others make similar criticisms, albeit in a different context, but the point is the same: harm reduction relies on prohibition for its sustenance; medicalisation is more radical, seeking to change policy. Medicalisation offers a different perspective and, according to Transform, distances itself from current policies.

Under a regulated drug market, the government will control and regulate the production and distribution of drugs (Transform, 2005). Production of drugs will be licensed and undertaken by pharmaceutical companies. There will be licensed medical practitioners and dispensing pharmacists controlling prescription and dispensing. According to Transform, there will be a new professional group called 'druggist and specialist pharmacists' who will be trained, licensed and qualified to vend certain drugs to recreational users, adhering to legal regulations and age restrictions. There will be licensed users where entry to that category will require membership, and regulations concerning the drugs purchased and consumed (2005, p 20). The effect *inter alia* of such a policy is said by Transform to be an improvement in public health with fewer drug deaths, and greater opportunities to control HIV and hepatitis C.

I hope that I have accurately stated the essence of Transform's position. Its programme offers one of the most comprehensive platforms for medicalisation. Taken altogether, I think it boils down to this (and I quote Transform again): there will be regulated drug markets according to the precepts above, there will also be restrictions as to who produces or manufactures the drugs, who can sell them, who has access to them, and when and where they can be consumed. Civil and criminal sanctions will still be incurred when rules are broken. Supporting this medicalised structure will be a team of medical specialists deciding on who gets what, when and where.

While one may accept certain merits to this proposal, some of its claims are overoptimistic. Transform believes that its policies will have a number of effects, some immediate, one of which is social and economic improvements in the drug-producing countries. Mary Ann Sieghert, the journalist quoted above, a strong supporter of Transform, sees the future of the producing countries in similar rosy terms: 'Unstable countries such as Afghanistan and Colombia, which have become almost ungovernable thanks to the distorting and corrupting effects of the drugs trade could sell their products legally to Western Governments for medical use' (*The Times*, 14 December 2006). (That they are ungovernable in part because high levels of availability lead to high levels of use, seems forgotten.) Can it really be that simple; cartels to change from illegal distributors to legal suppliers? Transform (2006, p 16) is equally bold: 'Legally regulated drug markets are a precondition for stability.' It is a claim based on very little evidence and is difficult to take seriously. It assumes that drug-producing countries such as Colombia, with a long history of terrorism, violence and political instability, will change as a result of the UK changing its supply system. In the scheme of things, the UK's share of the world market in cocaine is relatively small and hardly likely to produce more than a ripple were it to change its policies.

There are other defects in Transform's proposal. The most obvious is that it will not remove illegal supplies. In the absence of total legalisation, there will always remain a black market for drugs, and an illegal system to supply them. And with illegal supplies there will be offenders and sanctions as before. Transform admits this, saying civil or criminal sanctions such as fines will remain; it does not say who will impose and collect them. It is expected that there will be 'activities [which] occur outside of these legal frameworks, as is the case with ... underage sales of alcohol or cigarettes' (2006, p 15). In other words, 'some activities will remain prohibited' with 'restrictions as to who produces, can sell, and has access to drugs, and when and where they will be consumed'. It says: 'Public consumption could remain illegal' (2006, para 15). Would persistent rule breakers go to prison? Again not discussed. Where then are the advantages? And what is likely to change? Might this not produce a new form of prohibition, with new rules, regulations and sanctions? Might we be swapping one form of prohibition for another? Yes, of course.

Another omission concerns simple practical questions such as the likely facilities to be made available for the drug users. Will there be a

24-hour service, or will the new centres operate during office hours? This is neither a fatuous nor an inconsequential question. In my current research on the links between sex and drug markets (Bean, in preparation), the data show how interwoven and functionally dependent these two markets have become. Prostitutes working at night will often seek out the dealers, with the dealers being also available on what they call '24/7'. That leads to what the sex workers call going 'backwards and forwards', that is, the prostitute earns money, and immediately calls up the dealer. The drugs are delivered, and after the girl has 'scored' she goes back to work. She does this throughout the night at regular intervals. A few sex workers will wait until morning before seeking out their dealers but most will not. Given that these workers will earn and spend up to £300 per night, their earning power gives them a strong and important financial input into the drug markets. In fact, many drug markets are located next to 'red light' districts for that very reason. These prostitutes are not going to wait until the local centre is open or restrict their use to that provided by a regulated source (Bean, in preparation). They want illegal markets to be flexible, and offer a 24-hour service. I cannot see government-controlled prescribing centres offering a similar service.

Moreover, much of what Transform suggests has been tried before. Medicalisation was the favoured programme for the 1960s but overprescribing was rife. The failings of the British system in the 1960s were as much due to the medical profession as the users themselves. In 1964, an Interdepartmental Committee on Drug Addiction (the Brain Committee) was asked to advise the government on better prescribing of heroin to users following the rapid increase in the number of 'registered' addicts, from 470 in 1961 to 1,349 in 1966. It concluded that 'the major source of supply has been the activity of a very few doctors who have prescribed excessively for addicts (quoted in Bean, 1974, p 79). Barbara Wootton, in the House of Lords debate on the 1971 Misuse of Drugs Bill, thought that there were more than a few 'black sheep' as she called them. She thought there was a large number of grey sheep who

---

prescribed rather more than the average, albeit in some cases out of a mixture of good faith, carelessness or ignorance (*Hansard*, 1971, para 278). To stem the increase in use and curtail overprescribing, the Brain Committee recommended that treatment centres be introduced, where prescribing is permitted but only by specially licensed physicians. As a result, in 1968, and for the first time in the history of medicine in Britain, most physicians lost the right to prescribe heroin and cocaine to addicts. But also (and this is in favour of Transform), a few months before the treatment centres were introduced, the first illegally imported heroin arrived in Britain. Almost on cue, organised crime had arrived. The dilemma for all medicalisers is clear: insufficient control leads to overprescribing, severe restrictions lead to an illegitimate supply system.

Another lesson of the 1960s was that medicalisation did little to curb criminality. Addicts found that they had to feed themselves, pay rent etc and given their lifestyle this was often paid for by criminality. How else if they were addicted all day? At any one time in the late 1960s, about one third of those 'registered' addicts, that is, receiving drugs on NHS prescriptions, were in Brixton prison. Transform might say that the lessons of the 1960s have been learned; supplies will be more carefully monitored, and overprescribing reduced. One would hope so, but even if it were, one ought not expect too much from medicalisation, whether in its old or new form. The addict population now does not differ greatly from what it used to be. Now, as then, addicts make few attempts to control their habit, and now, as then, many live on the streets. Thus, the 1960s remain as a reminder that medicalisation is not new, and has within it certain fault lines.

That apart, a number of other questions remain. First, where does this leave crack/cocaine? This is the most difficult question for medicalisers, and few have given satisfactory and coherent answers. Transform avoided it, but Arnold Trebach confronted it. He said: 'Yes, I would legalise crack. It is a very dangerous drug, but the dangers of prohibition are on balance a greater threat to us all' (Trebach and Inciardi, 1993, p 110). (Husak, not a medicaliser,

47

also confronted it and concluded that crack/cocaine came close to satisfying his criteria as to substances 'that the state could justifiably prohibit'; Husak (1992, p 208.) The difficulty crack/cocaine raises for the medicalisers is that it is the exemplar of the recreational drug, having little medical value, is not addictive in the traditional sense of the term, that is, it produces none or few physical symptoms of withdrawal, but produces intense feelings of pleasure, which users say they feel an overwhelming desire to recreate. It is also known to promote violence. Is this to be prescribed, freely, and if so what can be the justification? If it is not then most of the medicalisers' arguments come to nothing for illegal markets will remain. Prescribe it and there is a furore among those who see it as a way of misusing scarce medical resources; ban it and we are back to square one.

Second, and related to this, what of the conditions under which prescribing should take place? Should applicants have to convince the medical practitioner that they are addicted to a specific drug, or would prescribing be on the basis of a request? And what then happens to those whose requests are refused? Where do they go from there? Presumably, back to the illegal supply system. That raises a related question, what of the novice or first-time user? Where did the drugs come from in the first place? And where will the novice get drugs and continue to get them until addicted? Or would the novice user go to a medical centre and ask to try some heroin, crack/cocaine or cannabis? If not, then that means first-time users must buy through the illegal markets – in the 1960s it was from 'registered' addicts selling surplus supplies, creating 'spillage', which explains why between half and two thirds of 'registered' addicts were in Brixton prison at any one time.

Third, does this, like all other forms of medicalisation, reduce the drug problem to medical dimensions – 'drug users are to be treated as patients, not as criminals'? Yet drug taking is not, and cannot solely be a medical problem, or even largely a medical problem. It involves social, moral, legal, criminological, and jurisprudential questions. To reduce it to simple medical proportions is not only wrong in principle, but also dangerous. Ignoring these dimensions

—

fails to understand what drives drug abuse onward, and similarly restricts attempts at holding it back (Dalrymple, *The Times*, 30 May 2008, p 21). That is why it is dangerous to reduce it to questions about how much should be prescribed, or who should run the prescribing system. People take drugs for many reasons, often to promote pleasure. Their use may later become a medical condition, but for many users treatment is not about promoting abstinence. Their dependence on and utilisation of the medical profession is more pragmatic, and less about changing status, more about getting their drug of choice when it suits them. To enclose them in a medical jacket might seem appealing, but I am not sure most drug users see it that way. Husak (1992, p 49) makes a similar point when he says 'that in the absence of a theory of disease, illness, injury or abnormality there is no firm basis to decide whether the use of a substance is medical'. He also says that policies to combat drug abuse will fail as long as the euphoria of use is discounted, and consumption explained solely in terms of deficiency of personality (1992, p 79).

A more basic question comes from Professor Neil McKegany (2008) who does not think prescribing heroin, or methadone, is appropriate. He sees it as a strategy beloved by top police officers and successive Home Secretaries, but is born of utter frustration at our seeming inability to tackle an escalating drug problem. He sees the basis of prescribing as: 'If you cannot stop addicts committing crimes to fund their drug habit then the next best thing is to provide them with the drugs that are the reason they are committing the crimes in the first place' (2008, p 71). He suggests that the logic may seem faultless, but it leaves the nagging question, 'Is it treatment or is it social problem prescribing?'(2008, p 71). And the answer must be the latter.

Finally, what is this 'legally regulated market'? If it means prescribing heroin or methadone, this is done already. If it means drug users taking their drugs in supervised conditions, then so well and good, as long as they can be persuaded to come to such centres. But they may not. What then? And how do you 'legally regulate' such a market, specifically a crack/cocaine market? Or the ecstasy market, or the cannabis market or all the other markets related to illegal drugs? How are these to be regulated when ecstasy, for example, is usually taken in clubs and bars? Does a 'legally regulated market' mean that all such drugs are to be made available whenever and wherever they are requested? If so, then we may finish up again with the worst of all worlds: high use and high crime, and a multitude of attendant social problems.

Decriminalisation

Decriminalisation, or depenalisation as it is sometimes called, is often used as synonymous with legalisation, since to remove legal controls is also to legalise. In the sense in which I use it here it is about restricting legal sanctions, which often means softening the impact or reducing the severity of legal controls. Decriminalisation is about assessing legal powers and legal sanctions, and where appropriate reducing or removing them.

There is no literature on decriminalisation as there is with the other ideal types, by that I mean no single supporter, or writer keen to pursue decriminalisation in a thematic form. Certain nuggets of information can be gleaned, which when put together can produce something approximating to a coherent proposal. Decriminalisation rarely turns out to be about removing sanctions, more about modifying those seen as inappropriate.

A typical decriminalisation argument was put forward by Barbara Wootton (1968) in her report on cannabis (a report by the Advisory Committee on Drug Dependence, but usually referred to as the Wootton Report). She spoke of the 'depenalisation' of certain offences (1968, para 90, see p 29). She said:

> It is our explicit opinion that any legislation directed towards a complex and changing problem like the use of cannabis cannot be regarded as final. For the foreseeable future, however, our objective is clear: to bring about a situation in which it is extremely unlikely that anyone will go to prison

for an offence involving only possession for personal use or
for supply on a very limited scale.

Michael Schofield, in his reservations, suggested that penalties for
possession offences should be related to the amount of cannabis so
that possession of 30gms or less should be a summary offence, with a
maximum fine of £50 for a first or subsequent offence. For possession
of any amount over 30gms on summary conviction by a fine not
exceeding £100, or imprisonment for a term not exceeding four
months, on conviction or indictment a fine or imprisonment for a term
not exceeding two years or both (see Wootton, 1968, pp 36-9).

   Decriminalisation, as offered here, provides a tariff where the
offences relating to cannabis are seen as deserving this or that
punishment. Barbara Wootton, without formally acknowledging
the presence of a tariff, clearly had one in mind when she saw the
possession and supply of small amounts of cannabis as not warranting
a severe sentence, while Michael Schofield wanted to be more precise,
spelling out deserts according to weights and amounts. They said
this irrespective of any utilitarian outcome, and ignoring accusations
that cannabis was a 'gateway' drug, that is, leading to more serious
drugs such as heroin – a topical debate in the 1960s and beyond.
The value and strength of the decriminaliser's position is shown here
for Barbara Wootton did more than affect the debate on cannabis
offenders; the report had a major impact on subsequent policy. Its
influence almost certainly stopped Britain going down the US route
with 'war on drugs' policy, and its horrendous sentencing practices of
'three strikes and you are out' – although, sadly, the 1994 Criminal
Justice Act comes close to changing that.

   Within any tariff there is a strong element of retribution, providing
a yardstick by which punishments can be measured against offences.
The problem with this and all desert-type arguments is that there
can be no agreement on what constitutes the appropriate desert. To
say that a certain punishment is excessive is to assert that there is an
alternative appropriate punishment, but there is no way of deciding
that, except by reference to another acceptable agreement about a

different tariff. If one person says that possession of cannabis does not deserve a prison sentence, and another says that it does, how are we to reconcile the differences? Usually resolution occurs by agreeing on what sentence fits the general consensus at the time, except that in Barbara Wootton's case she did more – she was instrumental in determining a new consensus.

Problems occur when the punishment is set below or above the consensus. In the UK, the maximum penalties for possession of cannabis were reduced in 2004 by downgrading it from a Class B to a Class C drug. Possession of cannabis in small quantities had already been decriminalised where for many years first offenders had been cautioned rather than prosecuted. Prohibitionists said this policy represented retreat, it implied cannabis was now legal, gave the wrong signal that cannabis was harmless and predicted greater use. In May 2008, as a result of much pressure and with the support of the Association of Chief Police Officers (ACPO), cannabis was reinstated as a Class B drug (see *The Guardian*, 3 November 2008; ACPO, 2008). A Home Office spokesperson, followed by the Home Secretary, said that the decision was based on its potential to cause harm and not on the prevalence of its use. First from the Home Office:

> We have to ensure that the classification of cannabis reflects the alarming fact that skunk, the highest-potency herbal cannabis, now dominates the cannabis market; and we must respond robustly to reverse the massive growth in the commercial cultivation of cannabis in the United Kingdom in the last few years. Reclassifying cannabis will help to drive enforcement priorities to shut the cannabis farms down. (Home Office press release, 2008)

Later, the Home Secretary said:

> Cannabis is and always has been illegal. It now dominates the illegal market in the UK and is stronger than ever before. There is accumulating evidence … that the stronger use of

52

> cannabis may increase the harm to mental health ... I make no apology for erring on the side of caution and upgrading its classification. There is a compelling case to act now rather than risk the health of future generations. (Home Office press release, 2008)

On a minor point of information, cannabis has not always been illegal: it has only been so since the 1925 Dangerous Drugs Act. That apart, it is interesting to see how the criteria have changed over the years. Barbara Wootton spoke about deserts; in contrast, the decision by the Home Secretary was about an 'increase in harms relating to mental health', that is, a shift from decriminalisation. Had the debate been conducted in decriminalisation terms, the outcome may have been different. Instead of the harms cannabis produces, why not ask directly what the possession (or supply) of cannabis deserves?

After cannabis comes ecstasy, where the suggestion is that it too should be downgraded from a Class A to a Class B – a Class A conviction for possession can result in a seven-year prison sentence while those who sell it can receive life imprisonment and an unlimited fine (see also *The Sunday Times*, 28 September 2008, p 22, 'Drug class war'). Oddly enough, the courts have long since sentenced those charged with the possession of ecstasy as if it were a Class B drug so decriminalisation in that respect would mean little change. However, the proposal to downgrade was initiated by reports saying that ecstasy was less harmful than alcohol and tobacco, supported by the former chief executive of the Medical Research Council who said that ecstasy was 'at the bottom of the scale of harm' and by the House of Commons Science and Technology Committee, but more importantly by the Advisory Council on the Misuse of Drugs (ACMD), a committee whose task is to advise the government. The Home Secretary said that she would not accept that recommendation, but in doing so raised questions about the government's rejection of expert advice, and about the way drug policy (read prohibition) can be driven as much by political considerations, media headlines and scare stories as by evidence.

—

53

A different strand of decriminalisation appeared with suggestions to the House of Commons Home Affairs Select Committee (2002a) for the reduction of sanctions where drugs are for personal possession. Drugscope said that 'its position in relation to users is a practical one, that in effect … drug use *per se* should not be criminalized' (2002, para 67). Turning Point, who told the committee that 'criminal procedures should no longer be initiated for the possession of small amounts of any scheduled drug' (2002, para 67), went on to say:

> Prison is never an acceptable environment in which to deal with possession. It does not serve a useful purpose for individuals or society….A criminal record makes education, employment and family relationships much more difficult at a crucial stage of a young person's life and they are more likely to learn more about drugs and serious crimes inside prison than outside it. (2002, para 68)

No one doubts this, and incidentally, as will be shown later, very few offenders go to prison for possession offences, but the proposal would produce many moral and practical problems. The House of Commons Home Affairs Select Committee thought it would send the wrong messages to young people, and the possible recruitment of new users. It might also give suppliers an incentive to seek to expand the user market. It would certainly engage enforcement agencies in a murky grey area between the user and the supplier, particularly in respect to small-scale social suppliers, and would add a further degree of confusion to policing drugs. It might also diminish respect for the law as it would embrace or offer a fundamental inconsistency, that is, that it is permissible to use drugs, but not permissible to supply them. The Committee said:

> Attracted though we are by the prospect of avoiding giving criminal records to otherwise law-abiding young people, we believe that this problem is better dealt with by reclassification…. We accept that to decriminalise the

> possession of drugs for personal use would send the wrong
> message to the majority of young people who do not take
> drugs. (2002, paras 67-70)

Nonetheless, there is, or ought to be, serious debate about what are and should be appropriate punishments for drug offenders, and whether the existing classification system should be retained. One aspect of the present system is the inconsistency in sentencing, where an offender in City A may get a fine for possession while a similar offender in City B gets a caution. Or worse, the length of imprisonment may vary from one court to another. Discrepancies in sentencing have long existed, and this is surely an appropriate matter for the decriminalisation lobby. Decriminalisation is or should be about fairness and justice. Included too should be an examination of the quality of the data on which policy decisions are made. The drug/crime figures are often faulty, with numerous errors not identified (our study of the data on traffickers in the Metropolitan District showed about 36% of the records contained errors). It may well be that sentencing practices are inconsistent, but without the data we shall never know. It may also be that certain groups are selected for undue punishment, but again, without the data we cannot be sure. The value of decriminalisation has always been to call attention to such discrepancies. It is easy to relegate decriminalisation to the outer regions of the debate, forgetting that it involves hard questions about tolerance, deserts and the implications of harm. These are moral questions and should be at the hub, not sent to some nether regions.

It is interesting to compare the decriminalisers with the legal moralists for on the face of it there would appear to be common ground. Legal moralists might see decriminalisation as a step in the right direction, but that would be as far as it goes. Assume that decriminalisers were successful and able to get the sentence for, say, possession of heroin down to that of, say, possession of cannabis. Would not that be an advance? At one level the legal moralist might applaud what they see as a partial surrender or compromise by the prohibitionist, but still insist that this is not what the debate is

---

55

about. Reducing the sentence may provide an important utilitarian advantage, but legal moralists do not see advantages in those terms. Legal moralism is not about reducing penalties. It is about the right to use drugs, which means that users should be no more fined than imprisoned. There may be fewer harmful consequences but that is not the basic objection.

What of harm medicalisation and harm reduction? How do these fit into a decriminalisation model? As used here, decriminalisation differs from medicalisation and harm reduction, being more confined to judicial and legal matters than about legal supply or programmes that reduce harm. Decriminalisation is at its best when requiring justifications for prohibitive sanctions, and when it casts a critical eye on the more hyperbolic features of prohibition.

In the following chapters, I want to move away from an examination of these ideal types to see how the critics of prohibition fare when faced with the implications of their proposals. In Chapter Four I deal with crime, the dominating feature of the debate. In Chapter Five I look at the proposals as they affect juveniles, and in Chapter Six at the likely consequences affecting the community, the individual user and the commercial consequences of these various proposals were they to be implemented. The final chapter involves an assessment of the situation that I have entitled 'Some concluding thoughts' but which are an attempt to put into perspective various proposals, and I ask what are the major questions to be asked of a rational drug policy?

Note

[1] Mike Ashton (2003) reports on results from Vancouver, which show a group of injectors with numerous personal problems including mental illness, which go with a lifestyle that includes depressing living conditions and recurring prison sentences. There was limited evidence for the effectiveness of needle exchange schemes even though one in five local injectors shared needles when they had no difficulty getting fresh supplies. Given the background of this injecting group – where experiences such as sexual abuse, suicide attempts and mental

disorder were common – this level of risk should be seen as successful, and its supporters would say, were harm reduction to be given more prominence, it would reduce that risk further. The literature on harm reduction is full of similar success stories.

4

Legalisation and crime

In this second part of the book I want to begin by looking at the links between drug use and crime. Not all drug users are criminal (except that the possession of an illegal substance is itself a crime), but some are, and the links between use and crime have dominated much of the debate. Almost all proposals boil down to one, probably two questions – how to reduce crime and how to reduce organised crime. Legalisers say that prohibition produces and promotes crime. They offer their solutions, some of which claim massive and immediate results, including a decline in the prison population; others are content to suggest that things might not turn out to be quite so dramatic. Prohibitionists accept crime as inevitable, but add that it prevents more than it creates; legalisers say they can reduce it.

Below I have listed nine major allegations that critics say occur as a result of prohibition. These are not in any order of priority, nor are claims made that this is an exhaustive list, or that it does other than set out the main contours of the debate. I want to see how they stand up to an examination.

(1) The drug trade is responsible for producing a massive increase in crime, which has become necessary to support the user's habit.

Nearly all criticisms of prohibition are predicated on the assumption of direct links between drug taking and crime. Nadelmann (1991, p 30), who appears to be speaking for others, sees a number of connections between drugs and crime, one of which is due to the relatively high price of illicit drugs. So, if drugs were significantly cheaper, which he asserts would be so were they to be legalised, the number of crimes committed by drug users to pay for their habit would accordingly decline. The extent of such a reduction is not given; but of course to be convincing Nadelmann would need to show this, or better still, show

how each reduction in price produces a corresponding reduction in criminality. This he does not do, saying that it is difficult to estimate the consequences of making drugs legal as legalisation is likely to spark high levels of curiosity, stimulated by the media. He calls legalisation a loose cannon as far as predicting the direction of drug use is concerned (Nadelmann, 1991).

Ignore for the moment the assumption that drugs would be cheaper if legalised, the first difficulty for most legalisers comes with their assertion of the link between drugs and crime. Given that almost all the research on drug use and criminality shows that many users were offenders before they took drugs – about 50% it seems – and that most will continue to commit offences whether or not they continue with their abuse, it is clear that no simple causal explanation exists (Bean, 2008). A major problem is to disaggregate all those offences that would have been committed from those committed as a direct result of being a drug user. This is an impossible task. Of course, many users claim they committed offences because of their drug taking, but this is to their advantage. It is less blameworthy to say they were propelled into committing offences by some unseen powerful hand than to admit that they were predatory criminals.

The second difficulty is determining to what extent there is a (sufficient) causal link between the drug and the criminality. There are three possibilities: drugs cause crime, crime causes drug use or there is no connection between them. In the first the link is straightforward whereby the drug itself is thought to be responsible – for example crack promotes violent outbursts – and less directly, that street heroin users are criminal for economic reasons, that is, to support a habit. The second is that crime causes drug use. This might occur where the offenders have surplus money, invariably from the proceeds of crime, and spend it on drugs. In the third there is no connection between the two morbidities. Determining which is correct is beyond the current state of criminological research; there remains the difficulty of determining or establishing such contingent influences. In an authoritative statement on the drugs–crime connection, MacCoun et al (2002) say that there is little evidence that drug use per se causes people to commit crime in some direct and unconditional manner. Much better to say that 'The drug crime link varies across individuals, over time within an individual's development, across situations, and possibly over time periods as a function of the dynamics of drug epidemics and, possibly drug control policies' (2002, p 2). There may be a necessary condition where criminality and drug abuse correlate but not a sufficient one. And to emphasise the point, Chaiken and Chaiken (1990, p 204) say in respect of preventing drug abuse that 'Preventing persistent use of drugs other than heroin and cocaine is not likely to reduce the numbers of persistent predatory offenders.'

The third difficulty is that consideration has to be given to the background of the users. This is best seen in longitudinal studies. These studies show that there is ample evidence that many persistent offenders have severe impediments to social functioning before they were users. David Farrington (1997) sets out the personal and social inadequacies of many persistent offenders, including impulsivity, low intelligence, poor parental supervision, socioeconomic deprivation and low educational attainment. Similarly, Lipton (in Inciardi and Harrison, 2000) in the US offers a list containing inadequacy (characterised by a pervasive feeling of an inability to cope), immaturity (unable to postpone gratification), vocational maladjustment (lack of employment skills), cognitive deficiency (overly suggestive and easily exploited), limited social skills (unable to function in a subordinate role: 'no one tells me what to do') and antisocial attitudes (demonstrates positive affective responses towards trouble, toughness, smartness, excitement, fate, and autonomy). Similarly Ethan Nadelmann (1999b) says that the principal determinants of destructive patterns of drug use are not the pharmacology of the drug but the setting in which it is consumed. He sees no setting more conducive to drug use than the combination of poverty and maladjustment. Of course, not all drug users come from this social background or display such limited skills, but many do, and they are often those who are also criminal.

—

Difficulties determining causal links can be seen in studies of prostitution – not, of course, a crime per se but prostitutes live in a world closely linked to criminality. Studies show that although almost all the street prostitutes were drug takers, some were prostitutes first (Faugier and Sargeant, 1997; Bean, in preparation). The most that can be said of the links with criminality is that many had criminal convictions, either for violence or for theft, before and during their career as prostitutes, but as to the causal connection between drug taking and prostitution this is difficult to determine. It is likely that for some, prostitution led to their drug habit rather than the other way round, they having money to spare, and they spent it on drugs, although clearly once a habit develops prostitution is used to pay for it. Many would most likely have continued to be prostitutes whether they had a drug habit or not. Most had an established deviant lifestyle long before they started drug taking: as young girls they were often truants, runaways or placed in care for uncontrollable behaviour.[1] (Drug taking among truants is about four times as high as among regular school attenders.)

Inciardi (1989a, p 263) puts the point forcibly for US street drug users: 'While drug use tends to intensify and perpetuate criminal behaviour it usually does not initiate criminal careers…. [T]he majority of street drug users who are involved in crime were well established prior to the onset of either narcotics or cocaine use.' This suggests that lifting barriers against the availability of drugs will not dramatically reduce the extent of crime; to suggest otherwise oversimplifies the drugs crime nexus. Modern drug use is typically one symptom of a complex series of social problems that cannot be addressed by simply legalising drugs and making them more available. Increases in crime in deprived areas are caused by the deterioration of informal and formal social controls within the immediate family, the education system and the social structure. Again, Inciardi asks, does anyone really believe we can solve these problems by legalising drugs?

Future studies may reveal the amount of crime committed by all drug users, and when they do, they may find less than described in conventional and popular media circles. More likely research will show a normal distribution with a bell-shaped curve where some users at one end commit no crime, with an equal number at the other end being actively criminal. Those in the middle – the bulk of the users – commit some crime but not a great deal. This bell-shaped curve, I suspect, could apply to all drugs, not just heroin. For these reasons alone, it is difficult to see a straightforward link between drugs and crime. My belief is that probably no more than 10% of crime is directly attributable to drugs, and of that figure it is mainly for reasons of crack/cocaine use and systemic crime (dealt with in No. 4) which is about protecting drug markets and collecting debt. If so, this undermines many of the arguments made by legalisers, although of course 10% is still a high number, and reducing it would be a valuable exercise.

(2) The drug trade has made large numbers of users criminal who would not otherwise be criminal. In an illegal market otherwise well-behaved young people are pushed into criminality. It means that drug use has massively increased the prison population.

The suggestion that the drug trade has made large numbers of users criminal who would not otherwise be so is based on two theories, the 'enslavement' theory and the 'out of character' theory. These are rarely articulated as such but implicitly support much of what 'everyone knows' about drugs and crime. James Inciardi (1989a, p 263) is a resolute critic of the enslavement theory, which he sees as basically misleading, supporting some of the more simplistic assumptions about drugs and crime. The enslavement theory suggests that because of the high prices of drugs, especially heroin and cocaine, many users, who would be otherwise law-abiding citizens, are forced to commit crimes to support their habit. Were criminal penalties to be removed, legalisers claim, three things would happen: first, the black market would disappear; second, the price of heroin and cocaine would decline; and finally, users would no longer have to engage in street crime to support their habit. This theory is predicated on the assumption that drug use precedes criminality, that users are offenders only because of

—

63

their habit, and were all forms of prohibition to cease then criminality would also decrease.

To the enslavement theory can be added the 'out of character' theory, also giving more than tacit support to the links between drug use and crime. Whereas enslavement suggests that criminality is a product of the drugs and the need for them, the out of character theory, although less dramatic, suggests that drugs change the personality of the users to their detriment. In both cases, drugs have become irresistible, the user's actions being determined by the craving, made worse by the high prices of drugs, and the perfidious nature of the control system. It means being trapped in a downward spiral of criminality. The out of character theory means behaving in a different way than hitherto, such as abusing close family members, or neglecting personal appearance or hygiene. In extreme circumstances it may mean committing offences for no obvious reason, becoming violent without any obvious provocation or damaging property needlessly. All occur in ways alien to the user's erstwhile character.

The enslavement theory, and the out of character theory, or its many variations, suggest that once the user is no longer enslaved by the drug and the pernicious nature of prohibitive controls, with its burdensome criminal sanctions, there will be release from the distress of drug use. Inciardi (1989a, p 263) suggests that it is a view that needs to be challenged. First, he says that while drug use tends to intensify and perpetuate criminal behaviour, it does not usually initiate criminal careers. Second, this theory assumes that people who are addicted to drugs commit crime only for the purposes of supporting their habit. Yet drug use is not the only reason why users commit crimes. They do so for many other reasons including to support their daily living expenses, such as food, clothing and shelter. Third, the theory assumes that they have to commit property crime to feed their habit. Yet it is possible to use heroin, be an addict, and still be a productive member of society – as happened to many 'registered addicts' in the 1930s (Bean, 1974).[2] Fourth, it assumes that if drugs are inexpensive, they will be affordable, and hence crime will be unnecessary (Miller and Gold, 1994, p 1075). Yet even if inexpensive, they may still not be affordable. On a rough-and-ready calculation, I think crack cocaine would have to cost no more than about 50 pence per 'hit' for it to be within the average user's price range and therefore affordable, but even then, other living expenses will still be high. Finally, it assumes that legalised markets will allow users to obtain all the drugs they want and all problems of crime, ill-health and unhappiness will suddenly go away. This is to insulate drug users from their criminality, while conveniently laying the blame on the system of control. So, either the drug is to blame, or those who decide how the drugs are to be supplied are to blame, but not the people taking them or committing the offences. It is a neat way of shifting responsibility.

Moreover, the enslavement theory is based on the assumption that most if not all drug users wish to remain drug free and crime free, and that if the right sort of incentives were available, and the wrong sort of barriers removed, all would be well. Perhaps some do, but many do not, and often those who do will only do so when they no longer want that lifestyle, involving arrest, prison, homelessness and so on. Until then, they like so many others prefer to control their addiction, rather than be rid of it. Typically, they will have a history of several years of drug use, including many failed treatment programmes. Abstinence is not always their immediate aim.

No one disputes that the enslavement theory has some merits. Some users are 'enslaved', and some behave 'out of character', and were changes to be made in, say, prescribing practices, there might be benefits. Some individuals die as a result of drug impurities, and some would benefit by changes in government controls and the regulations that define legal substances. But as shown in the 1960s when pure heroin and other drugs were freely available on prescription, together with sterile equipment, careful use rarely occurred, and there were still many deaths.

A recurring theme is that legalisation 'would remove the obligation of giving criminal records to large numbers of young people arrested for drug use who are, in all other respects, law abiding citizens'

—

(House of Commons Home Affairs Select Committee, 2002a, para 68). It was not made clear in the Home Affairs Select Committee document who these were, and how many 'would not otherwise be criminals'. No data are ever presented, nor any evidence given to support this claim. Nor, it seems, did the Committee challenge this assertion. It is not clear why these offenders are to be protected. What is it about drug offences that should set them apart? We do not say the same for 'otherwise law-abiding citizens' who happen to have, say, stolen property, have been caught shoplifting, have committed assaults or been dangerous drivers. Yet we have already moved towards making that distinction for drug use. In our eagerness to promote a meritocracy we have inadvertently produced a group of public entertainers called 'celebrities' who, where they are involved in drug taking, are protected by their status from the moral condemnation reserved for others. Rock stars, models and the like are the most obvious examples, but so too are some middle-class users. There was an outcry in 2007 when the Metropolitan Police Commissioner said he would pursue and prosecute City cocaine users. If drug laws are to be used in order to protect selected groups of users there is something seriously amiss.

As to that expected reduction in the prison population, how realistic is this? Again I want to use the data provided by the Transform Drug Policy Foundation as this organisation has been bold enough to give figures (Transform, 2006). It says: 'Anecdotal evidence suggests that between 50% and 80% of prisoners are inside for crimes relating to fundraising to buy illegal drugs' (2006, p 10). It also says that legalisation would mean that 'property crime and the prison population would be halved', adding that street prostitution would be ended (2006, pp 6-10 and p 16). Halving the prison population would mean a reduction of up to 40,000 prisoners, which is a massive reduction, and would lift a huge burden from the criminal justice system, reduce overcrowding immediately and leave the criminal justice system with spare capacity. It would produce the most dramatic change in criminality ever recorded. Yet it is difficult to take these claims seriously, made worse by the absence of any detailed explanation as to how Transform arrived at this conclusion. The figures seemed to have been produced, conjuror-like, out of the lobbyist's hat.

How realistic is it to suggest that 40,000 prisoners are in prison as a direct cause of their drug use? Two sets of data would be required to support this contention, the first is available, the second is not. For the first, there are data on those drug users convicted under the principal Act – the 1971 Misuse of Drugs Act – of a drug offence, possession supply and so on. This, however, accounts for a relatively small number of drug offenders – and incidentally includes some who are not users, that is, traffickers who do not use the drugs. As far as the prison population is concerned, of those convicted for a drug offence in England and Wales over the last decade, only about 10% were sentenced to immediate custody, and that figure has remained fairly constant. In 2003, a total of 73,170 offenders were dealt with in court for drug offences, the number of offences amounting to 87,730. Of these offenders, 8,770 were sentenced to immediate custody, with an average sentence of 29 months (Home Office, 2005). Those receiving custodial sentences were almost always convicted for supply, with the longest sentences reserved for the most extensive suppliers. Rarely were offenders sent to prison for possession offences (only about 4%) and even more rarely if the drug in question was cannabis. Offenders charged with possession were more often cautioned, especially if the amounts involved were small, with cautions accounting for almost half of all prosecuted drug offenders. Those not cautioned but prosecuted were most likely to be fined (see Bean, 2008, chapter 3).[3]

The second group are users and offenders, where their Index offence is not a drug offence. There are large numbers of these, and presumably Transform sees this group as providing the major piece of evidence for its assertion that 'between 50% and 80% of prisoners are inside for crimes relating to fundraising to buy illegal drugs' (Transform, 2006, p 10). Numerous studies show that large numbers of offenders – about 60% – admit to taking drugs prior to or during the commission of their Index offence. But that is not all Transform claims. It wants to assert a more direct causal connection.

The problem is that the evidence does not support that, for the reasons given above, that is, the evidence provides only a correlation, not a causal link. Transform would need to show that most or all those offences were caused by drug taking, and in such a manner as they would not have occurred otherwise. This it cannot do. It can reasonably assume that some were, but how many and for what reasons it cannot be certain. Therefore its assertion of such a link must remain an untested hypothesis.

Transform is on more certain ground in respect of women offenders, where drug trafficking has been responsible for an exploding women's prison population. The number of women in prison has doubled from 1996, many serving sentences of six years or more, almost all from overseas, usually Jamaica, and many serving sentences for trafficking. In spite of this increase, the overall figure remains low, there being only about 4,500 women prisoners compared with over 75,000 men. The numbers are too small to add significantly to the grand total required by Transform.

Taking an overview of the data, it is difficult to determine who these large numbers of users are who would not otherwise be criminal, or find support for the claim that drug use has 'massively increased the prison population'. There has been an increase in drug offenders and in the number of offenders using drugs, but linking drugs and crime in a causal way is beyond the capability of current research.

(3) The drug trade has helped create and develop organised crime syndicates and made enormous profits for them. The introduction of crack/cocaine has made a bad situation worse.

There is much evidence for this. Milton Friedman was correct when he said that the role of government has been to create and protect the drug cartels. This somewhat unorthodox comment is intended to show how prohibition has created its own criminality. Friedman says that there would be no cartel without prohibition, although we may dispute what is meant by 'protecting the cartel'. Presumably he means that prohibition created the cartels, and their existence is sustained by it.

There is evidence that a small number of traffickers are able to dominate the markets, and others, developing the so-called 'middle markets' are able to control large quantities of drugs. At the international level, some organisations are drug specific but others will actively move into other illegal markets as and when profits determine. It is easy to play up or play down the existence of these organisations; some were active before drugs became lucrative (for example, the Mafia, Triads) but some only because of drugs. Mike Levi and Lisa Osofsky (1995) dispute some of the more extravagant claims of profits made by, and on behalf of, the traffickers, but there is little doubt that for some the profits are huge.[4]

While the drug trade may not have created these organisations, it has helped develop and sustain them. This has led some legalisers to point to parallels and claim that alcohol prohibition in the US in the 1920s was responsible for introducing and developing gangland violence and organised crime. However, the oft-portrayed view that prohibition fostered and promoted organised crime is one of those myths itself fostered and promoted by Hollywood. Its guns and gangster depiction is wildly inaccurate. It is worth giving the details of crime and health matters during the prohibition period, about 14 years in all, to emphasise the point. Kleber and Inciardi (2005, p 1392) say that there was a higher rate of homicide between 1900 and 1910 than during prohibition and organised crime was well established in cities before then. Mark Moore confirms this. In a chapter entitled 'Actually prohibition was a success' (Moore, 1992a), Moore points out that alcohol consumption declined dramatically during prohibition. Cirrhosis death rates for men were 29.5 per 100,000 in 1911 but reduced to 10.7 in 1929. Admissions to state mental hospitals for alcoholic psychosis declined from 10.1 per 100,000 in 1919 to 4.7 in 1928. Arrests for public drunkenness and disorderly conduct declined 50% between 1916 and 1922. For the population as a whole, the best estimates are that consumption of alcohol declined by 30% to 50%. And confirming Kleber and Inciardi's point, Moore says that violent crime did not increase dramatically from 1900 to 1910 but remained constant during prohibition's 14-year rule; it may have become more visible and lurid during prohibition but it existed before and after. Why then did prohibition fail? Not because of crime rates, but because alcohol was so embedded into American cultural life that it was impossible to prohibit it further. And what of organised crime? Prohibition did not create it, and did not develop it, but did little to reduce it.

The introduction of crack/cocaine has certainly made a difficult situation worse. This is not in dispute, and is a failing of prohibition. Yet it shows too a main fault line in the legalisation case. It is a question that stands above all others; what to do about crack/cocaine? Crack, the drug designed to produce the ultimate pleasure, and the very emblem of the modern recreational drug culture, is the drug least able to fit into the legalisers' scheme of things – although other drugs such as 'ice' (methamphetamine) could be included. James Q. Wilson, a prohibitionist, has no such difficulty in opposing any move to legalise crack/cocaine. He says of drug use generally that it degrades human character, but of cocaine it debases life and alters one's soul (quoted in Husak, 1992, p 67).

Some legalists have been bold enough to enter the fray. Transform (2007) says that the simplest solution would be for powder cocaine to be sold or prescribed from specialist pharmacy outlets under strict conditions. As prescribing cocaine is already possible in the UK it says that no change in the law would be required, although it suggests that prescribing guidelines would need to be updated. What then for crack? Transform says that 'since making smokable crack/cocaine from powder cocaine is a simple kitchen procedure and one that is impossible to prevent, so dedicated crack users may continue to procure it, even if it were not directly available' (Transform, 2007 p 42). It concludes that 'Ultimately however the pragmatic reality remains that if someone is determined to use crack it is preferable that they have a supply of known strength and purity and do not have to commit crimes against others or prostitute themselves as a means to buying it' (2007 p 41). So, we are to prescribe cocaine but regret that it is to be used as crack.

I cannot see how this is a satisfactory position. I cannot understand why we should be expected to endorse and fund the supplies of a recreational drug, which may lead to some measure of violence, but even if not, then it will be taken as a pleasurable risk. And at considerable cost to the NHS? Most medicalisers, including that of the Rolleston Committee, saw the prescribing of drugs to those who were addicted, including maintenance prescribing, as being a short-term measure to get users over the period until they were ready to seek treatment. It was justified on the basis that addicts became sick people, but their initial foray into drug use was pleasure. It was only in the 1960s that the so-called 'British system' was transformed into a free-for-all supply system when any physician could prescribe any drug of choice, including cocaine, or for that matter tincture of cannabis and huge quantities of methedrine. The Second Brain Committee (Ministry of Health, 1965) rightly recommended that such a prescribing circus should not continue. Transform seems eager to return to that.

If there is to be a return to this free prescribing system then who picks up the pieces afterwards? Estimates vary but it seems that about 10% of crack users go on to be serious compulsive users. Yet these would all be supplied and their subsequent health problems presumably treated by an NHS system that is already unable to meet demand from other patients, including those with terminal conditions. What sort of system is that? For crack/cocaine we could also read 'ice', a drug more potent, more powerful and able to give more intense pleasure than crack. And for any other drug some home-made chemist may in future come up with, having no obvious medical value but able to produce pleasure of that or a greater intensity – are such drugs to be supplied too? How about if I say I have no interest in crack, but rather like expensive motorbikes. Would these also be prescribed on the NHS? After all, they give me pleasure and are risky to have. What makes crack different?

The House of Commons Home Affairs Committee (2002a, para 147) wanted to 'redouble efforts to extinguish the supply of crack cocaine'. But that is not easy; I am told it is possible to stand in some parts of the Andes, and as far as the eye can see, and in whatever direction one looks, all there is to see are coca bushes. There is never going to be a shortage of supply. As far as recommending changes, the Committee said it saw 'no prospect for compromise' (2002a, para 148). It noted that few witnesses argued outright for legalisation and said that 'We leave it to those who do argue for general legalisation to explain how this could be justified given that, unlike other illegal drugs, crack can trigger violent and unpredictable behaviour' (2002a, para 148). Milton Friedman's point that the development of crack was solely down to prohibition needs to be noted (Friedman and Szasz, 1992, p 66) but having produced it there is no easy way back. However, his view that 'violence is due to prohibition and nothing else' (1992, p 66) does not fit easily with the facts. Crack itself is capable of producing its own form of violent behaviour. For that, and other reasons, it is not easy to justify legalising a drug as potent as this.

In summary, there is no doubt that the drug trade helped develop if not create organised crime syndicates and made enormous profits for them, and no doubt crack/cocaine has made a bad situation worse. As to the solutions, none suggested seems appropriate: the use of crack/cocaine defies them. Whether we like it or not, prohibition promotes the only way forward as far as crack/cocaine is concerned.

(4) The drug trade has produced its own systemic crime where dealers are required to protect their markets. As the trade is itself illegal, violence is the favoured form of market control. The drug trade has also led to an increase in corrupt practices, notably where informers are concerned so that any chief constable wanting to devote limited resources to anti-corruption measures would usefully direct them to the drug trade.

Again, there is a good deal of evidence to suggest that the drug trade has produced its own systemic crime where dealers are required to protect their markets. And there is little doubt that in the trade illegal violence is the favoured form of market control. In this the legalisers are correct. What is in doubt is whether crime, including violence, would decline in a legalised drug market. Inciardi (1999, p 56) thinks it might actually increase, blaming it on a likely increase in use. He says that removing the criminal sanctions against the possession and distribution of illegal drugs would make them more available and attractive and therefore create a large number of new users. That would inevitably result in a greater number of dysfunctional addicts who could not support themselves, their drug habits or their lifestyles through legitimate means. For many that would mean an increase in street addicts with crime their only alternative.

In fact the position could be worse. With an increase in the use of crack/cocaine, more violence might occur, not just by the dealers but by the users. If the markets were not fully legalised then illegality will continue, with the criminality created by these markets running alongside the extra criminality created by an increase in users. Not for the first time are legalisers accused of creating a possibility of the worst of all worlds.

Legalisers are on more firm ground when they accuse prohibitionists of promoting an increase in enforcement practices, which if not corrupt, border on the unsavoury, and which some see as a threat to civil liberties. These include various enforcement strategies, such as the use of informers, buy and bust operations, controlled deliveries and so on. All are said to be underhand strategies, although all are legal and covered by stringent regulations. The organisation Liberty is a forceful critic of such activities:

> [T]he practical consequences of current drug policy also creates substantive infringement into basic civil liberties. The nature of trying to police and fight crime on such levels has led to significant increases in draconian and restrictive laws and policing methods.... Thus intelligence and surveillance have been developed and are used to fight the 'War on Drugs'. Such methods of policing are by their very nature intrusive and restrictive on civil liberties, in particular Article 8 rights but also Article 6 of the European Convention on Human Rights. (Liberty, 2001, paras 9, 11)

Liberty is not correct, or rather the inferences offered are slightly misleading. Some of the methods are intrusive, and informers, undercover operations including buy and bust and controlled deliveries are all invasive methods of obtaining convictions (Billingsley et al 2001). But they were not invented to deal with drugs, they existed long before the drug trade, and not only for victimless crimes. Informers, undercover operatives, and listening devices have been used against armed robbery, terrorism and paedophilia and presumably Liberty has no objection to those. Nor does the use of these devices violate the European Convention on Human Rights (ECHR). Parliament has successfully dealt with those objections through the 1984 Police and Criminal Evidence Act (PACE) and the 2000 Regulation of Investigatory Powers Act (RIPA) (Neyroud and Beckley, 2001). The former developed rules of exclusion for evidence that appeared to be tainted by informers, and the latter provided the police and other public authorities with a legal framework that will enable them to use covert methods without violating human rights. This legislation may not meet with Liberty's approval but other like-minded organisations (for example Justice) appear not to dissent, recognising the need for such legislation and regulations.

On the other question of the best place for a chief constable to place limited resources to deal with corruption there is no doubt that concentrating on the drug trade would produce the best results. Drugs, low in volume, high in value and bought and sold almost entirely in cash, provide an attractive area in which corruption can flourish. The interactions between police officers and informers provide ready-made opportunities for corrupt officers to exploit (see Billingsley et al, 2001). Furthermore, the drug trade is imbued with treachery, and with profits high then temptations are common. Yet it is easy to have a one-sided view (Clarke, 2001). Corruption is not confined to the police and drugs.

(5) The drug trade has produced a massive cost in enforcement, which could be more usefully spent on treatment and prevention. On cost alone the amount is difficult to determine but comes to many billions of pounds, especially when the full cost of enforcement is included alongside the cost to the courts, the criminal justice system and interdiction.

There is no doubt that in order to operate a fully-fledged prohibitionist policy, enormous resources are needed for enforcement, prosecution and incarceration. It is not possible to arrive at a figure of the cost; estimates put it in billions of pounds – I have seen a figure of £1,026 billion cited of which two thirds is on enforcement (Transform, 2006). Nor is it possible to assess whether this money is well spent as costs have rarely been systematically evaluated, and expenditure rarely audited with a cost-benefit analysis. If prohibition is to be taken seriously, enormous resources must be devoted to it. Legalisers say that the cost is much greater than the amount spent; hidden costs such as institutionalised corruption, betrayal, chaos and terror need to be included (Bakalar and Grinspoon, 1984, p 112). Richard Stevenson (1994, p 53) says that legalisation would provide a massive saving for the Exchequer, simply because the cost of law enforcement would be reduced.

The prohibitionist defence is to acknowledge that costs are high, but counter this by stating that legalisation is also costly, or worse, that it might actually increase costs. There is no doubt that legalisation would provide savings on the costs of interdiction, but then only if crack/cocaine was made legal, otherwise interdiction costs will remain. We cannot assume that legalisation will be cost free. We cannot assume that there would be an improvement in health or a reduction in death rates should drugs become legal. The repeal of prohibition might be the salvation of the criminal justice system but could produce an unacceptable burden on the NHS. Or it might reduce some types of crime but at the expense of reducing the health and social functioning of drug users and their children. Rarely have legalisers spelt out the costs of their programmes, and this has been a serious omission.

(6) Prohibition has produced a massive increase in use, but legalisation might make things worse.

The claim by legalisers is that prohibition has led to an increase in use, and that legalisation would reverse this. Supporters of legalisation see repeal as the most obvious way of reducing the number of users. On the other hand, prohibitionists say that this grossly oversimplifies a complex situation, and in this they have the support of Inciardi and McBride (1991), who think that removing criminal sanctions would make drugs more available, more attractive and therefore create a large number of new users. Both sides claim that there will be an increase in use, and each blames the other. The case for the legalisers is made by the existing data, and the massive increase in convictions over the years (see Bean, 2008, chapter 3 for a discussion on this). The case for the prohibitionists is that there would be an increase should legalisation occur.

Inciardi (1999, pp 56 and 1990, pp 85-6) puts the case for prohibition. He says that no one knows for certain the extent to which legalisation would increase the number of addicts or whether such a strategy would undermine the integrity of our society. Few would deny that the greater availability of, and easier access to drugs would increase drug use beyond current levels. Would there be such an increase? Ethan Nadelmann, with disarming honesty, says that 'All the benefits of legalisation would be for naught if millions more Americans were to become drug abusers.' And later, that 'It is impossible to predict whether legalisation would lead to much greater levels of abuse' (Nadelmann, 1991, pp 37, 41). He recognises that prohibition may actively keep the drug problem lower than otherwise, and without prohibition there might be an increase, although prohibition itself is two-edged: it may discourage some users, but encourage others. The legalisers' case is straightforward. It says that prohibition has failed and will continue to fail for all the reasons described above. The evidence is said to be clear: there has been a steady increase in use over the past decade and there is no sign that it will stop. Legalisation becomes the only rational alternative.

What sort of increase are we likely to expect if legalisation occurs – 10%, 20% or more? There is little evidence on which to base predictions. The number of drug users who are dependent when the drug is illegal tells us little about the numbers, or percentage increase or decrease, when they are legal. Assume, however, that there would be an increase, what would be acceptable? And if it reaches an unacceptable level, what to do about it? Return to prohibition? Or find some other way? Re-prohibition would be a difficult and expensive option with no likely short-term effects.

To talk of an increase in this blanket way assumes that all drugs are the same, have the same appeal and produce the same social effects. But the likely increase in cannabis use may be greater than for heroin, and would be of less significance than a similar increase in heroin or crack/cocaine use. Nadelmann (1995, p 329) agrees that there will be an overall increase but plays down the dangers, believing that a well-designed and implemented policy of controlled drug legalisation would not yield costly consequences. He accepts that different problems would arise for different drugs, and accepts too that dangers associated with cannabis are less than for heroin. He tries to soften objections by saying that for heroin the problems are not as great as many think (1995, p 329). Yet assume a 10% increase in heroin and crack/cocaine use – a not unreasonable assumption. This would produce an accompanying set of problems, some long term, some short term. The former would be an increase in chronic use, the latter would be pressure on public health and treatment services. What if that led to a 10% increase each year, how long before rates of use and chronic use became unmanageable?

For some drugs the rates of increase may be higher than the 10% expected. Assume crack/cocaine would be higher, then we would have a problem of some magnitude. Of course, these calculations might turn out to be wildly inaccurate, grossly overstating the case, but they might not. And if not, what then? Alcohol use is already at levels where governments are expressing concern. If we had a problem the size of alcohol it would be an unmitigated disaster (Kleiman and Saiger, 1990, p 542). But that is quite likely. After all,

—

we are unable to deal effectively with alcohol use, especially so-called 'binge' drinking among young people. Kleiman (1993, p 8) makes the perfectly valid point that until success is achieved in imposing reasonable controls on the currently licit drug of alcohol, the case for adding another is hopelessly speculative. Erich Goode (1999, p 119), however, thinks that the group that would benefit the most would not be the new users, but the heaviest users: 'Think what a paradise ... it would be for them, they could get their supply from both barrels – legal and illegal sources.'

What of the economic liberals and the legal moralists? Szasz (1996) has no interest in debating an increase in use, it being a matter of the rights of adults to choose whether to use recreational drugs. Friedman (1992) is more circumspect, as are the legal moralists, yet as Husak (1992, p 172) repeatedly states, his primary aim is to protect moral rights, not solve the drug problem. He hopes and expects that drug users will show restraint over time, place and quantity. He says that 'this is not to require the impossible' (1992, p 255), hoping that a successful programme plus informal controls might emerge. But if they didn't, then what?

And if there is an increase, will it fall on specific areas of the population or be a general increase? Some critics say that it will fall disproportionately on inner-city areas, on the young and on minority ethnic groups, especially those with a poor work record and an equally poor social prognosis. Some critics in the US say that legalisation would represent a programme of social management and control, legitimating the chemical destruction of an urban generation and culture (Inciardi and McBride, 1989, p 270). These are strong words indeed.

(7) The drug trade encourages young people to enter it because of the excitement it offers and the appeal to riches beyond their current earning power. It undermines their chances of being productive and useful members of society. Drug dealing helps promote them into a delinquent subcultural world from which it is difficult to extricate them.

In many respects this is true. The lack of skills required to enter the drug world, as a dealer, and the ease of transportation of a high-profit commodity, are likely to be attractive. Not only that but there is a certain excitement about an illegal activity, and some young people are drawn to that. Whether they would lose interest were drugs to be legal is a moot question. Stevenson (1994) thinks they would. It is also true that the drug trade offers some young people opportunities to earn money way beyond what they could expect in legitimate occupations according to their age and qualifications. 'It's the best job I'll ever have,' say young dealers, and they could add 'or ever be likely to have'. These riches may not be long-lasting. If deductions are made for time spent in prison, or from the time and money spent protecting their markets, or developing new ones, and the constant fear of losing their hard-won gains, the overall effect is that most dealers earn little more over a five-year period than they would in the employment most commensurate with their qualifications. Dealing enriches in the short term but impoverishes later. In an earlier study in Nottingham (Bean and Wilkinson, 1988), dealers themselves often lamented that 'dealing doesn't last'. They made their pile of crazy money but invariably lost it as quickly, whether from their own drug use, through burglary by other dealers, or being 'busted' by the police most often on information from another dealer.

In one sense, being a drug dealer does undermine the chances of being a productive member of society. Drug markets are violent places where the overall effect is that those working in them become more frightened of each other than of the police. They operate in a Hobbesian world where no rules apply except those made by themselves, and other dealers, aimed to serve their mutual interests. Once initiated into that world it becomes difficult to extricate themselves or function in any other way. Husak (1992, p 55) takes a different view, hoping that removal of the enormous profits might motivate dealers to seek a more honest living. He might have his hopes dashed, but he is certainly correct to say that the obscene profits make a mockery of the work ethic, where the existence of a lucrative black market for drugs may have contributed more to deterioration in education than the drugs themselves.

—

(8)The drug trade has led to disrespect for the law by many who no longer believe the rhetoric of the dangers of many of the prohibited drugs, and such disrespect is itself dangerous in a democracy as it undermines the basis of our democratic freedoms.

This is a difficult matter to determine. Claims are made that drug laws lead to disrespect for the law, and of course disrespect on a significant scale would be dangerous to democracy. But how to determine it? In the early days when the 'scared straight' model was used, when police officers tried to frighten schoolchildren about the dangers of drugs, this led to disrespect for the police as the young children knew rather more than those giving the talk. That approach has been abandoned. The House of Commons Home Affairs Committee (2002a) concluded that there was no clear evidence that restrictions on possession deter the misuse of drugs. Conversely, there was no clear evidence that they failed. The numbers so influenced are difficult to determine, but one of the reasons given for not taking drugs was their illegality – other reasons were fear of being addicted, loss of control and pressure from friends and family (Lipton, 1989). It is not clear which of those was the most important.

(9) The drug trade has helped undermine the social fabric of producing countries such as Colombia.

This is an oft-stated accusation against prohibition. Karel (1991, p 90) claims that with legalisation there would be little incentive to continue illicit production since drugs would no longer be an irrationally valued commodity. Transform (2006, p 10 and 16) claims that prohibition produces political economic and social instability in drug-producing and transit countries. It claims its solution would remove the corrupting and destabilising influences of illegal drug profits and drug cartels. It also says that illegal drug profits help fund and arm paramilitary groups, guerrilla groups and terrorist groups across the globe, fuelling violence and conflict (2006, p 11). Richard Stevenson (1994, pp 54-5) holds similar views: 'The principle merit of legalisation is that it would retard the spread of corruption and criminality which threatens the political and legal fabric of whole societies.'

—

The drug cartels of South America have accumulated significant political influence, and their resulting wealth and coercive potential has made them a severe threat to the economic institutions. Damage is not restricted to the economic environment; it extends to political institutions where the proliferation of sophisticated weaponry among traffickers and the ease with which they can undermine democratic institutions are commonplace. That is so whether in South America, South East Asia or elsewhere, but it is in South America that these factors are most often combined. There are also disturbing signs that the traffickers' influence has spread to smaller economies throughout the Caribbean, undermining the political and economic institutions in what were already fragile nation states. Drug cartels are organisations aimed at producing maximum profits, using any opportunity to undermine existing democratic institutions. Whenever they take over legitimate businesses, or develop shell companies, the effect is to reduce the viability of those companies. The traffickers' aims are to produce sham companies through which they can promote their activities.

I do not want to become too involved in the internal and international politics surrounding trafficking except to say that the situation in Colombia is probably out of control, and that some neighbouring countries come close to that. The question here is would the cartels wither away, as Karel (1991) suggests? Would legalisation remove the mass production of drugs, restore order to the producing countries and stamp out the traffickers? The answer is almost certainly no. It is unlikely they would give up their lucrative empires that easily. There would still be opportunities to sell some of their products as there remains a market for the drugs to be sold in legal outlets, for example for the production and supply of government-purchased opium. However, there would still be a market for illegal transactions whether from juveniles, novices or others not wanting to purchase or receive drugs through legal markets. It would not be difficult to undercut official outlets. Simply by altering purity levels, traffickers could maintain profit margins (McSweeney et al, 2008, p 10).

An assessment

The nine allegations listed above cover most of what is contained within the debate on crime. Speaking generally, some of the accusations have been sustained, for example that relating to the growth and spread of crack cocaine, as has the cost of prohibition, but others have not. Some allegations are difficult to prove, for example the deterrent effect of legislation where there is no real evidence either way, there being no evidence that laws deter, but neither is there that they do not. The result is a mixed bag, except that there is no doubt that prohibition has led to the growth of illegal markets. What remains unclear is whether legalisation would do otherwise.

Notes

[1] To some (Dalrymple, *The Times*, 31 August 2007, p 19), the solution is not about repealing the 1971 Misuse of Drugs Act but to double the number of prisons and pass much longer sentences on those sent to prison, for without this, Britain will continue to be a failed state. 'The class of victims of crime is much larger than the class of perpetrators as most offenders commit many more crimes than those for which they are convicted. And the victims themselves too often are from the poorest areas of our cities and it is the level of crime that makes life in those areas such torment.... Failure to imprison criminals is thus a weasely betrayal of the poor by the well to do middle classes who do not want their taxes used in this way.... Millions of crimes a year are committed by people already on probation or just released from prison after short sentences, and such sentences let every victim know that the State does not take victimisation seriously' (2007, p 19).

And again in *The Times* (7 December 2007), Dalrymple returns to the same theme: 'The consistent failure to immobilise criminals properly has been a wicked and sanctimonious betrayal of the working class by middle class intellectuals who have dressed up a refusal to spend tax money on the preservation of law and order, especially in poor areas, as compassion and understanding for the working class.' Further, 'It is often pointed out that the recidivism rate of prisoners serving short term sentences is 70 per cent (actually, this is the reconviction rate, the offending rate is probably nearer 100 per cent). But this is an argument for drastically lengthened sentences not for leniency.' And 'It is easy to demonstrate that millions of crimes a year are committed by people already serving community sentences; thus failure to imprison properly is one of the main causes of crime in our deeply criminalised country.'

[2] In the 1930s, many addicts came from 'medical and allied professions' and by controlling their habit were able to remain in full-time employment, with, in many cases, their habit known only to the Home Office. Not even to their wives and families. The physicians would inject themselves morning and night, before each surgery, with no inclination to increase the dose. They lived up to that old maxim 'take alcohol and you get drunk, take heroin and you stay normal'. The modern addict chooses a different lifestyle.

[3] Moreover, some offenders hide their drug taking from researchers or the courts, fearing that disclosure would lead to a longer sentence – especially pregnant offenders who might expect a remand in custody for a health check (incidentally were drugs to be legal that might not change: the courts have a duty to protect the unborn and newly-born child) – while others exaggerate their dependency hoping for sympathy and a lighter sentence. Research on drugs and crime continues to be an imprecise activity. One prostitute in my current research says she always tells the solicitor, the psychiatrist and the probation officer that she is a drug addict: "It helps them explain the prostitution, makes them feel good and I get a lighter sentence."

[4] The 'cartel' is a South American concept, defined as an association of traffickers and money launderers working together to supply drugs, mainly cocaine. The South East Asian supply system is different, run by individual entrepreneurs, often from Hong Kong, who arrange supply and delivery through complex international networks. These networks are as adept at smuggling cars as drugs, and will, if the profits are sufficient, smuggle anything worthwhile. While heroin may be the

favoured drug, being small in quantity and high in value, others that are more bulky such as cannabis will be smuggled as required. There are other supply systems for heroin (the Turkish connection being one) and other drugs have their own separate systems: ecstasy comes mainly from Holland, 'ice' from South Korea via the US (see Bean, 2008).

5

The special problem of juveniles

Too often the debate about drug legalisation seems to exist as if juveniles – young people under the age of 18 – do not exist. Yet drug use invariably begins between the ages of 15 to 17 – sometimes even younger, especially among offender populations (HM Government, 2004). Moreover, the peak age of criminality is around the same age, 15 for boys and 16 for girls, so that if, as is often asserted, drug abuse and crime go together, there is empirical evidence to support it, at least in terms of the ages at which they begin (Farrington, 1997). Patterns of drug use seem also to follow patterns of criminality. That is to say, very few heavy drug users start drug use after the age of 21, in the same way that very few offenders begin their criminal career after the age of 21. A persistent feature of the data on juvenile offenders is that almost all adult offenders were juvenile offenders, and almost all serious adult drug users were juvenile users (West and Farrington, 1977). Not always, but more often than not. The extent of drug use tapers off in the same way that criminality tapers off after the age of about 28 to 30. However, there are differences – the ratio of male:female criminality is about 5:1, whereas for drug use it is about 3:1.

These basic facts provide an important dimension to the debate. If, as stated, drug abuse commonly starts among 15-year-olds, alongside other problems such as crime, then age, and its attendant problems, becomes an important factor. Yet, age has often been ignored, whether by policy makers, prohibitionists or legalisers. Husak (1992), for example, provides an exemplary critique of prohibition as it affects adults, but is strangely silent about children. He is concerned to 'understand the best principled reasons for denying that adults have a moral right to use any or all of recreational drugs' (1992, p 5) but says little about whether children are to be excluded. So too Ostrowski (1990), who produces an equally coherent argument on similar lines – that adults have a right to self-ownership of their bodies – but like Husak does no more than briefly mention the problem of juveniles. Transform talks about controlled availability producing a significantly improved environment for reducing harm (Transform, 2006, p 27) and hopes that 'positive education and supply constraints' will inhibit their use, but does not spell out what these would be.

We know that the groups of children most at risk of drug taking include the homeless, young people abused through prostitution, teenage mothers, and young people not in education, employment or training. These children are also most likely to come from deprived areas of our cities (HM Government, 2004). The problems they present are new in the sense that drug abuse is a relatively recent phenomenon, but not in the sense that social problems and deprivation are entwined. The juvenile justice system bears a heavy burden – over 50% of young offenders in custody reported Class A drug use in the past year, among the highest of any risk group (HM Government, 2004).

The impact of the child savers

We have inherited from the child savers, that band of energetic American Protestant women of the late 19th century, the principles on which much of modern juvenile justice is based (Platt, 1969). They saw the need to save children from the evils of the slums, and the crime and destitution that was an inevitable part of the lives of neglected waifs. But these were no sentimentalists. 'Child saving' required love, discipline and training, not always in that order. The child savers' aim was to turn these children into productive members of society, and if that required a period of intense training away from home, then so be it. If on the other hand it required a less harsh approach then that too should be provided. It all depended on the child's character and their response to being saved. But saved these children will be, whether they, or their parents, wanted it. The result has been a set of unspoken but highly influential principles on which modern juvenile justice rests. They may not always be articulated but they remain embedded within the deeper recesses of most statutes. Below I describe three – the plasticity model, the reserve capital model and the family model – although for 'family' also read 'local authority care'.

First the plasticity model. The child savers believed that children were more amenable to discipline than adults; their characters remained sufficiently pliable or plastic to suggest they might learn from experience. Speaking generally, and probably excluding older adolescents, we still retain that view, believing children's characters to be not fully formed, or fixed, and accordingly offer more chances of promoting change. Children are thought to be impressionable, and as a result not sufficiently mature to assess harms, which for these purposes include the dangers and impact of drug use. Nor are children able to assess fully the implications of drug taking, and are not likely to judge the immediate, short- or long-term impact of their actions. Research on the main motivations for taking drugs consistently shows that curiosity, peer group pressure, excitement and risk taking are the factors likely to appeal to young persons. In contrast, motivations for resisting drug taking in adults are a lack of interest, health concerns, fear of loss of control, illegality, fear of addiction, and not being enjoyable. Another attribute of plasticity is that it allows children to be more amenable to treatment, or should do. Successful treatments for adults for drug abuse tend to be lengthy, lasting at least 60 days, but placing children into treatment programmes, and away from peer group influences, would expect to take less time but be equally effective.

Second, the children of today are the adults of tomorrow – this is the so-called 'reserve capital' argument. The child savers saw the need to invest in today's children for they are our future and the future of our society is in their hands. The reserve capital model requires that children reach their potential. The Earl of Lytton in the parliamentary debate on the juvenile court in 1908 stated the reserve capital argument when he said: 'The Bill is concerned not only in a spirit of tenderness and affection for the child's life but also with real interest in the future welfare of the State' (quoted in Bean, 1981, p 125). And James Callaghan 60 years later said: 'the aim (of the 1969 Children and Young Persons Act) was to prevent the deprived and delinquent children of today becoming the deprived, inadequate, unstable and criminal citizens of tomorrow' (quoted in Bean, 1981, p 125). In the House of Lords debate on the 1971 Misuse of Drugs Bill, Lord Windelsham wanted legislation lest we 'should put at risk our interest in the welfare of a substantial part of an entire generation of young people' (*Hansard*, 1971). Harms done to children's education which damage their future also damage society's future, and drug use is known to have that damaging effect. Children who use drugs tend to have poor educational attainment, tend to truant, be disruptive when in school, and drop out of school early. Their poor educational attainment is invariably followed by a poor work record, such children finding it difficult to accept industrial discipline. Not being amenable to discipline, they fail to develop adequate self-discipline. There are harms also to the child's physical development; children who take drugs tend to have health problems associated with a disruptive lifestyle, and if they inject they can have infections and other diseases in injection sites and elsewhere.

Third, the family model. Children need to live and develop within the confines of an adult family structure and relationships. This was an important platform of the child savers and its relevance today cannot be ignored. We often forget that in order to assist children, their immediate families and key adults must also be involved. Without adult cooperation, attempts to deal with the child can be undermined. Yet attempts to reintegrate drug-taking children within the family place strain on family relationships – I keep saying this but it is important, ask anyone whose child is a persistent drug user. Children who take drugs tend to be disruptive and receiving cooperation from the family is a prerequisite for success. An American programme for drug-abusing children was predicated on two major assumptions: get the family on board, and get the children into school. If that meant taking and meeting them then so be it. Successful treatment of children depended on their integration into those key institutions.

The influence of the child savers on contemporary systems of juvenile justice is apparent. They emphasised the importance of 'saving' children through the law by imposing on parents and schoolteachers, or indeed any adult acting in *loco parentis*, duties to provide the child with care and support. Accordingly, the law formally imposes on parents a duty not to neglect a child, expose a child to moral danger or allow a child to be beyond control. In addition, there are legal requirements relating to the child's attendance at school. The rights of the parents are not absolute; the state has powers to take control over children, whether through wardship proceedings or through the care system, should there be evidence that children are likely to suffer significant harm. They can be placed in the care of the state. This may involve handing the care to others, a local authority perhaps, or in extreme cases to other parents through adoption. A typical example would be where young children are brought up within a family of drug users, frequenting and growing up in a world of parental injecting, surrounded by discarded needles and subject to physical neglect. These children will be seen as endangered, and rightly brought before a Youth Court, which sitting as a civil court, will determine whether they are in need of care and protection. So too with drug-using pregnant women. In the US, this can result in the mother being detained until she gives birth, followed by the likelihood that the child will be placed in statutory care, and maybe offered for adoption.

The aims of the care system have been to provide children with surrogate families, offering them care and control. Laudable as such aims may be, sadly, we too often fail. Local authority care has regularly become a breeding ground for delinquency, prostitution and drug abuse. In my research on the background of street prostitutes in Nottingham (Bean, in preparation) a large number, about 45% of the hundred or so interviewed, had been in care, many beginning their prostitution in care (including rent boys). This finding is supported by other research (Sanders, 2005).[1] More disturbing is that many started their drug taking while in care, but most of those children had a history of behavioural problems well before that, often before going into care. It is a bleak picture; children who have been in care for 12 months or more can expect to remain there. This has led to legislation in the US where all children in care for over 12 months are automatically put up for adoption. The impetus behind this legislation is that the state is not prepared to wait for some mothers, mostly those with a drug problem, to be ready to care for their children again. To do so is, regrettably, often to wait forever. This legislation with the threat of adoption pushes some parents into action, and for those it does not, they may never be ready.

The child savers have provided the basis for much of contemporary legislation. Recent legal developments have slightly amended some of those earlier precepts, making modern forms of juvenile justice (for juveniles or children, the terms can be used interchangeably) considerably more detailed and sophisticated. Yet the basic principles are retained, for example that children are children, that they mature at different stages, and become increasingly responsible for their actions, yet still require protection from those who would harm and exploit them. In the UK that paternalism is such that the state takes responsibility to protect children over and above what their parents might wish. UK law also provides special provisions for its vulnerable citizens, children, people with learning difficulties and people with mental health problems being the most obvious groups (for example through the use of procedures such as Appropriate Adults during police questioning). In this it is in full agreement with John Stuart Mill who said that his precepts on negative liberty applied only to those in full possession of their faculties, children being exempt; and with utilitarians such as T.H. Green who said that juveniles were unable to have an understanding of the nature of rights concerning the public good, neither did they have an awareness of the omission or violation of such rights. Bentham thought that children were too young to face consequences and future events, and were not able to understand the full implications of future actions. All accepted that the rights of children were not the same as those of adults. Faced with the modern problem of substance abuse it is likely that all would have agreed that, if paternalism was justified, then it was surely justified for children.

What children can or cannot do

Making decisions for and on behalf of children involves a delicate assessment of responsibility, based on the rate at which children mature. Maturity is related to, but not wholly dependent on, age, although as a general rule, older children are more able to accept responsibility than younger children. It is unlikely that we would countenance drug taking by a six- or seven-year-old, but we may be less concerned when that person has reached adolescence. A 17-year-old bordering on adulthood would justifiably claim to have fewer paternalistic impositions than a younger person. The problem is that there is no magical age at which full responsibility arrives, nor any magic to produce, or determine, that responsibility. It makes no sense to blame that six- or seven-year-old if that child does not know right from wrong, or a 17-year-old if development has been retarded. Lawyers in England and Wales talk of being *Gillick* competent. (This is a developmental concept based on perceived levels of maturity; *Gillick v West Norfolk & Wisbech Health Authority & Dept. of Health and Social Security, 1985*.) Although this particular case related to the prescription of a contraceptive pill to a juvenile without her parents' consent, the principle is relevant to what is discussed here. A decision to respect the child's wishes, in whatever context that might be, would be based on the maturity of the juvenile, not necessarily on the basis of age. (General Medical Council, undated). How one recognises maturity is another matter. We are left with the private judgements of adults who are required to make the decisions – parents, school teachers, the police and so on.

Paternalism is about protection but is also about control, which for children means by the legal system and parental responsibility. Legal control, parental control and responsibility are bound together. The law sets out in a general way what children can and cannot do. First, that children generally have fewer rights than adults and are often held less accountable. Children cannot normally undertake contractual obligations and are not normally entitled to their own earnings, nor can they manage their own property. Moreover, children younger than certain statutory limits are not allowed to vote, hold public office, work in various occupations, drive a car or be sold certain kinds of reading material, quite apart from what their parents might wish. Nor can they buy tobacco and alcohol. For adolescents, we restrict their recreations, whether through reading material, or where they can go, about what they can see in the cinema, or about what they can wear.

Second, as far as the courts are concerned, children under the age of 10 cannot be prosecuted for a criminal offence, but they can be dealt with under care proceedings in a court sitting as a civil court. Those children appearing before the Youth Court on criminal charges are subject to certain procedures prior to trial. The names of children and young persons cannot be given publicly without the permission of the court, and if convicted, children and young persons have recorded against them 'findings of guilt' rather than 'previous convictions'. These procedures are based on the assumption that children require protection for their actions.

Third, underpinning these legal provisions is a theme or principle that in all civil proceedings for juveniles, when the court determines questions with respect to the upbringing of the child, the child's welfare shall be the court's paramount consideration (1989 Children Act, Section 1). Court decisions are aimed primarily at improvement, so that the child may learn from any decision the court may make. The Youth Court sitting as a criminal court punishes children in order to appeal to feelings that in later life act as a censor for moral behaviour. (For a discussion on the punishment of children, see Bean, 1981, chapter 4.) We punish children who take drugs in order to encourage them to believe that drug taking is wrong, and to believe that drugs are harmful and not in their best interests. In contrast, we punish adults because they deserve it, to deter them and others, and only occasionally to reform them. Important as is the principle that the child's welfare is paramount, in practice, and taking a narrow view, decisions will tend to be dominated by the age of the child and *Gillick* competence. The 'welfare of the child' is more relevant for a

10-year-old than a 17-year-old, and the court's decisions will reflect that. Possession of a Class B drug for a 10-year-old will presumably be viewed with more concern than for a 17-year-old. For children who commit offences, the court has a wider range of sentences, and the justifications more specific. Rehabilitation is emphasised, with deterrence and retribution accorded less importance.

Fitting contemporary requirements: prohibition and legalisation

To what extent are the various proposals able to fit contemporary requirements? Prohibitionists have no difficulty answering questions about which drugs children should be allowed to take, or in what form. Their view is that all drugs are prohibited whether for children, adolescents and adults. Nor would they have difficulty justifying this according to the precepts above. They would accept that children's characters are pliable, but would add that this can work both ways: pliable in the sense of being easily influenced, but on the other hand capable of responding to training – with of course the fear of being wrongly influenced. Adolescence is a time of experimentation; but it can and often means embarking on activities that can have long-term unpleasant results.

Nor would prohibitionists find difficulty with the second precept, that of the reserve capital argument. As part of its drug strategy (HM Government, 2002) the UK government said in terms highly reminiscent of James Callaghan 30 years before that the 'central aim ... is to prevent today's young people from becoming tomorrow's drug users' (HM Government, 2002, p 1). In a different publication it repeated the point, saying that it wanted more emphasis to be placed on early interventions with vulnerable young people who are most at risk, especially those 'starting down the road of substance misuse to becoming problematic drug users' (House of Commons, 2002a, p 3). Two years later, the government set out some of the dangers in which many children found themselves. It cited a report from the Advisory Council on the Misuse of Drugs (ACMD), which estimated that between 200,000 and 300,000 children in England

and Wales have one or both parents with serious drug problems (HM Government, 2004). Some treatment centres are already seeing the grandchildren of drug users seeking methadone maintenance, and in my current research on prostitution a number of young working girls are supporting their addicted parents and siblings; the parents themselves were juvenile drug users (Bean, in preparation). Attacking these dangers, including this form of inherited dependence, would be a priority for prohibitionists seeking to preserve society's future.

There is no difficulty either with the precept that children require protection. Stopping them taking drugs is self-evidently protective, which in this context includes prevention. Lord Windlesham in his justification for prohibition said: 'Where children are involved there is a danger of abandonment and neglect' (*Hansard*, 1971). The UK government said that 'Reducing drug use by young people particularly the most vulnerable is central to the Government's updated national drug strategy.... We need to prevent drug misuse and the harm it causes to young people through more effective drugs education, prevention and early intervention' (HM Government, 2004, p 1). In its reply to the Home Affairs Select Committee (House of Commons, 2002b, p 3), the government made clear that it will target all young people through education and advice to warn them of the dangers of drugs. It said: 'The protection of young people is vital' (House of Commons, 2002b, p 3), going so far as to raise that spectre of dealers who prey on them. 'The Government will consider making dealing to minors a serious offence. Those who deal near schools will be sentenced severely. We will support parents and families to help them cope with the effects of addiction' (House of Commons, 2002b, p 3). Incidentally, rarely do children start drug abuse as a result of adult dealers selling drugs outside the school gates. Almost all start through the encouragement of their peers. Punishing the seller of course eases some of the moral and political doubts about children, especially as the symbolic value of the criminal law is greater if it is directed at the seller rather than the user (Bakalar and Grinspoon, 1984, p 116). These doubts can be further eased if the seller can be seen as forcing the drugs on an unwilling and vulnerable user, that is, a child or young person. Blaming and prosecuting sellers, however, is not the answer.

In spite of the claims by the UK government, as a prohibitionist, it has been criticised for falling short, or failing to deal with juvenile drug use, whether by failing to prevent, contain or treat it. Critics say that the law does not prevent it; it may even attract young people, offering the excitement of illegality. This and the increase in use these past decades suggest that prohibition has been less than successful. Worse than that, prohibition pushes young people into a subculture of drug use, creating a bias or incentive in favour of riskier behaviour and more powerful psychoactive effects (Nadelmann, 1991, p 22). The ease at which drug taking becomes an acceptable way of life for many young users, especially in the slum housing estates of our cities, is, say the critics, a further indication of the failure of prohibition. Yet legalisers are open to the criticism that they too have failed to deal adequately with the problem of juvenile drug abuse, often appearing to relegate it to a matter of less importance.

Milton Friedman (Friedman and Szasz, 1992, p 79) said that we should prohibit the sale of alcohol to children, whereas Thornton (1998, p 655) says that with perfect legalisation there would be no prohibition on the purchase of drugs by minors. There would, however, have to be some self-imposed regulation by the sellers and the parents who are the legal guardians of their children, and responsible for their behaviour. Stevenson (1994, p 61) sides with Friedman: 'All drug reformers agree that the sale of drugs to minors should remain illegal and that the law should be enforced strictly'.

If we take Thornton's position that there should be no restrictions on juveniles, it means that every drug in whatever quantity and potency should be available for purchase by anyone, regardless of age. That leaves little common ground with the child savers. Thornton has no wish to usurp parental responsibility and little interest in concerning himself with forcing young people into treatment. He might be concerned to protect society's future, the reserve capital, but would still leave this to parents. If this is so, there is an urgent set of moral problems afoot. What happens if parents and schoolteachers do not abide by the rules, do not exercise restraint and do not protect society's future? What if there is a massive increase in use, as there might well be? What then? Do we leave the matter there? Or does the state step in, and protect the child as it would under existing legislation? Or should it stand aside and allow and extend the freedom to buy and use recreational drugs as these young people please? Presumably there would be no restrictions on alcohol or tobacco otherwise it would be bizarre, and wholly hypocritical to have restrictions on some drugs and not others.

There is little doubt that Thornton supports state laissez faire; he wants to give parents the right to make decisions for their children. Were that to be so it would require primary legislation in the UK. In spite of what Thornton and other free marketers might wish, the state exercises rights of surveillance, both formal and informal, over children and young persons. At the formal level that may mean direct involvement through wardship or care proceedings, and at the informal level through the support offered by social workers through social services departments. Social workers also have powers to operate their own supervisory forms of control through the sentencing powers of the Youth Court. Again, to change this would require primary legislation, and whether a case could be made for such a change, especially as it would apply only to drug abuse, is difficult to say. Thornton and others like him also seem to ignore the fact that juvenile justice must fit certain demands. We invest in children a mixture of expectations, paternalism and hope for society's future, and rightly say that they require special attention and care. Of course, the cut-off point at which they can be prosecuted, or be held legally accountable, is arbitrary; and this creates a special problem where the juvenile's age is borderline, but this does not affect the main point about the special provisions required. And why stop at drugs? Would Thornton approve of a free market for the sale of knives to juveniles, or allow them to ride motorcycles without crash helmets as long as they had parental approval? Presumably yes, but with what results?

The less ardent free marketers, such as Stevenson, want to impose restrictions on children buying drugs. Stevenson (1994, p 61) says that 'All drug law reformers agree that the restrictions on the sale of drugs to minors should be strictly enforced.' Or that parents 'have to learn risk management' (1994, p 61). None says what to do if parents do not exercise that control. Nonetheless, for Stevenson, and Friedman, the upshot is clear: not wanting children to buy drugs means they are imposing another form of prohibition, however slight and albeit on a selected group – the young. Thornton avoids this trap but does so at the risk of producing large numbers of juvenile users, whereas Friedman and Stevenson would simply swap one set of regulations on prohibition for another. Why? They do not say, but presumably would not disagree with the child savers, that the characters of children are pliable, that children are society's future and that they require protection. What that means for their programme, and the likely outcome, is not clear, but for the children little would change. Children, as before, will find that they can only buy drugs from illegal sources.

For the rights theorist, the same question remains: are juveniles to be prohibited from purchasing substances, or are they to be allowed to do so in the same way as adults? Husak (1992, p 243) says that his arguments about rights do not apply to juveniles, stating that to his knowledge no moral legalist has gone so far as to propose that adolescents and adults have equal rights to use drugs recreationally. He thinks that adolescents lack the moral right to use drugs recreationally, but fails to point out the implications of that. If they have no right to use drugs then where do they get them from? Not the same place as adults, such as chemist shops or other retail outlets as permitted by some legalisers, only from illegal syndicates. That again puts things back to square one. The organisation Liberty is in a similar position. Having stated that it wants 'complete deregulation of all drugs', it then backtracks, saying that it accepts that there are some circumstances that will require regulation and in some cases the criminalisation of certain aspects of supply and consumption of drugs. 'These would include for example the supply of drugs to minors' (Liberty, 2001, para 8). Again, back to square one.

Is it possible to find more detailed arguments from the other ideal types – harm reduction, medicalisation and decriminalisation? First, harm reduction. On the face of it there is no conflict. Harm reduction, by definition, is about removing or relieving harm and that must include harm to adolescents as well as adults. The International Harm Reduction Association (2008) includes the drug takers' families as falling within its remit. It is not clear if harm reductionists give any priority to adolescents, but one can see that they might. Adolescent drug use can, and often does, lead to long-term adult use, with associated high death rates and high rates of infection.

Prevention would qualify as harm reduction. It could operate at two levels – individual prevention and general prevention. In order to prevent drug taking at the individual level, as a harm reduction strategy the aim would be to reduce the amounts used, but preferably to encourage children not to use a drug at all. Ideally, of course, the aim would be to promote a general prevention programme aimed at avoiding all harms associated with its use, but this may not be possible, in which case the aim must be more limited, directed at reducing harms among current users (Hawks and Lenton, 1995). The trouble is that some strategies aimed at reducing individual use can have the opposite effect and increase the extent of harms. For example, strategies aimed at reducing the use of, say, crack/cocaine among young users by getting them into treatment might produce a weakening of general deterrence, and so increase levels of use overall. Or strategies at reducing criminality among young users might create the impression that drug use was acceptable. Whichever one chooses is a matter of values as well as utilitarian consequences (Moore, 1992b, p 137).[2]

What of medicalisation? Transform believes that legally regulated and controlled markets will offer a far greater level of protection to vulnerable groups than the chaotic unregulated illegal markets we have today. These regulated markets will 'prevent early drug use as a public health initiative and as part of a wider harm reduction approach' (Transform, 2006, p 49). It is not clear how such prevention will occur, but to call existing illegal markets 'chaotic' misunderstands the controls and regulation offered by offender networks. Nonetheless, the question remains, how will medicalisation, or rather that version offered by Transform, provide facilities for juveniles? The answer is that it is difficult to say as there is nothing offered except the decision to prescribe by medical personnel based on the clinical decisions of the juvenile patient's habit. However, the Liberal Democrats who seem to be close to Transform, said at their 2006 conference: 'The last thing we would want is for any child to take drugs' (*BBC News*, 18 September 2006).

Richard Karel (1991), a medicaliser, attempts to answer his critics who say that medicalisers rarely produce concrete proposals, and even more rarely produce proposals for juveniles. He claims benefits for juveniles in his proposal, which he suggests would eliminate the association between drugs and an underground subculture. Removing the profit motive would, he says, reduce the incentive to employ children in the drug trade (Karel, 1991, p 89). But he admits that critics are probably correct in assuming that it would be impossible to keep drugs out of the hands of children altogether (1991, p 89). He says: 'In discussing regulation and distribution of narcotics, the implicit assumption is that these substances be made legal only for adults with the restrictions noted.' He goes on to say: 'Drugs would not be made available for children. Age limits could be either 18 or 21' (1991, p 89). That does not get us very much further.

A major difficulty with this and all arguments that suggest the law should apply only to children is that there is nothing in common law jurisdictions that provides for separate laws for children. We do not have criminal legislation that applies only to juveniles, and there is nothing in the 1971 Misuse of Drugs Act about age. To introduce it would require the legal system to be reconstructed, and it is difficult to see how this could be justified, or what sort of flood gates would then open. Presumably, one could construct an

—

argument to justify this change, perhaps along the lines that existing legislation is inappropriate as drugs pose unique problems. But then what of theft, burglary, violence or motoring offences? Could not similar arguments be made for them? Of course, the Youth Court provides facilities whereby children and young persons who commit offences under the 1971 Misuse of Drugs Act, or under any other criminal law legislation, are dealt with separately, but this is a matter for venue and proceedings. They may be sent to the Youth Court rather than the Magistrates Court for trial and sentence but only according to the requirements of juvenile justice practice. This point, straightforward though it may be, provides limits on what can be achieved without recourse to primary legislation.

A possibility would be for the 1971 Misuse of Drugs Act to apply only to juveniles. If so it would mean that the Act would be retained, specifying that it was an offence for juveniles to possess and supply a range of drugs. Is this any better? First, what would be the age cut-off point? Assume 18, in which case a young man approaching his 18th birthday could be prosecuted, but had he waited a few more days he would not. Of course, as said above, all cut-off points are arbitrary, whether for voting, driving a motor vehicle or reading certain literature, but here the cut-off point is about being prosecuted, a more serious matter. There are additional complications where levels of maturity are considered. An adolescent may be more mature at 17 than his 18-year-old companion, in which case the youngest will be prosecuted and the other not. This legislation would produce a catalogue of injustices, a legal minefield and more problems than it solves.

Another possibility would be to exclude juveniles from criminal legislation but retain care proceedings. Would this improve matters? In some ways it would, but in others not. On the positive side, the principles of children's welfare would be retained but it would create numerous legal and social problems. Additional legislation would be required, including an offence of 'selling or helping children procure drugs'. If addicted, would children be allowed to receive maintenance drugs, legally prescribed? Presumably some drugs such as crack/cocaine would not be legally available to children, but assuming they were legally available for adults, this would create legal difficulties that would not be easily resolved.

Finally, what of decriminalisation? There is little in decriminalisation programmes that affects juveniles. There is the persistent contention that changing cannabis from a Class B drug to a Class C drug will reduce the criminal involvement of juveniles, but little more is offered. Or that juveniles are being encouraged to take drugs because of the excitement promoted by making drugs illegal. Or that some juveniles are being made into criminals who would not otherwise be offenders. But all these are more speculative than anything else, and have been more usefully dealt with in Chapter Four.

An assessment

Assessing the position overall, it seems that almost all proposals – Thornton's is the exception – would prohibit the use of drugs to juveniles. They may do so in varying forms, some being more prohibitive than others, but the differences are often marginal. In practice they will make juveniles subject to prohibition as before. This is not an unimportant point, for if prohibition is to be retained for juveniles, using criminal or civil proceedings, then many existing problems remain. Husak (1992, p 244) comes to a similar conclusion when he says that those theorists who promise that legalisation will bring an end to the evils of the black market must be deluding themselves, since a limited war will still have to be waged on behalf of adolescents. Claims that legalisation for adults will ultimately benefit children through a sort of trickle-down effect, such as reducing the criminal impact, or removing the stigma attached to substance abuse, may or may not be realised.

None of the ideal types listed above offers a satisfactory solution, and more likely would produce more problems than they solve. For example, legalisers such as Stevenson (1994) say that under prohibition, children fare particularly badly. He then proposes a system where drugs are to be made legal for adults only, and assumes that that solves the problem. Karel says likewise (1991, p 89) that substances should be made legal only for adults. He then adds that while it would be impossible to keep drugs out of the hands of children things would be better 'because the elimination of the profit motive would reduce the incentive to deliberately employ children in the drug trade or otherwise entice them into contact with drugs'. If children are not allowed to take drugs, there will still be an illegal system, leaving the profit motive intact. Sliding over the problem in this way helps nobody. The only real solution of course is to reduce demand, which means exercising parental control alongside legal control. And if the latter then we must accept Husak's warning about deluding ourselves if we believe that we can avoid waging a limited war on behalf of adolescents.

In conclusion, there is little in the legalisers' plans to suggest that they are doing much about drug use by children, except to say that legalising drugs should not be construed as encouraging use. Stevenson, it will be remembered, thought that under legalisation 'drug use will become boring', but said little to suggest this might be so. That rather typifies many of the legalisers' proposals: they rely too often on hope that were they to change policies for adults, similar improvements would appear for children. That they may not is cause for concern.

Notes

[1] The extent to which drug taking has already changed much of the landscape of prostitution is becoming clear, leading to re-examination of earlier roles. For example, traditional 'pimping' has largely vanished; the drug and the dealer are the new pimp, controlling the sex worker's behaviour, but without the forms of control exercised earlier. This new pimp does not control a number of girls but is no less demanding. The new 'boyfriend' is there but more often in a supporting role rather than a controlling one. She shares her earnings with him, he protects and supports her and she helps buy his drugs (Bean, in preparation). Most working girls have their first drug-taking experience as a result of peer pressure, or as curiosity, or as excitement, and continue with their habit still believing 'addiction will never happen to me'.

[2] We may not always be adept at finding ways to prevent juvenile drug use but sometimes it seems as if we actively encourage it. In the UK, a non-governmental organisation – Lifeline – was heavily criticised by the Home Affairs Select Committee (House of Commons, 2002a, paras 205, 207) for what it called 'crossing the line between accurate information and encouraging young people to take drugs'. A pamphlet addressed at young people advised: 'Don't get caught in the first place. Don't be blatant or obvious and remember parents search bedrooms and coat pockets. If you do get caught don't expect your parents to understand.' Lifeline's defence was that it did not know how to stop young people taking drugs. It therefore decided to look at what was possible. Unsurprisingly, the Select Committee was not impressed.

6

The community, the personal and the commercial

The implications of the legalisation of drugs go well beyond the impact on crime, or the position of juveniles; they enter the very nature of society itself. I want to look at the likely impact of the various proposals, beginning with the wider picture, then looking at the implications legalisation might have for individual users, finally turning to the way the commercial institutions are likely to respond. I want to begin with an assessment of the prohibitionists' fears of a threat to society and the individual user.

The community

In the US, James Inciardi and Duane McBride (1991, p 49) put the matter this way when they say: 'Considerable evidence exists to suggest that the legalisation of drugs would create behavioural and public health problems to a degree that would far outweigh the current consequences of drug prohibition.' James Q. Wilson feared that without prohibition 'we will have consigned millions of people, hundreds of thousands of infants and hundreds of neighbourhoods to a life of oblivion and disease' (quoted in Lowinson, 2005, p 1397). Or again, he said that prohibition was justified, or rather legalisation was not justified, because 'to the lives and families destroyed by alcohol we will have added countless more destroyed by cocaine, heroin and whatever else a basement scientist can invent' (Wilson, 1995, p 338). Inciardi and McBride see drug use as a mode of adaptation to the disadvantages of ghetto life, in which case they say that without prohibition, drug use would produce a nightmare for the underclass. 'Legalisation', they say, 'becomes an elitist and racist policy, and would increase levels of dependence in the ghetto where it would serve to legitimate the chemical destruction of an urban generation and culture' (Inciardi and McBride, 1989, p 279). Strong stuff indeed, and a quote worth repeating.

In the UK, support for the prohibitionist view is found in Lord Windelsham's speech to the House of Lords in the Second Reading of the Misuse of Drugs Bill, later the 1971 Misuse of Drugs Act. He said that the guiding principles in the government's mind were that society has a right to use the criminal law to protect itself from forces that may threaten its existence as a politically, socially or economically viable order. He further justified prohibition: 'We cannot stand by and watch appalled and uncomprehending while a disabling and unnatural habit flourishes in our society' (*Hansard*, 1971). Again, strong words, offering a similarly fearful scenario were legalisation to occur.

Lord Windelsham hints at something more important, more disruptive than activities that evoke mere dislike. Notice he talks of 'forces which may threaten its [society's] existence' and of 'a disabling and unnatural habit [that] flourishes in our society'. These offer a distasteful future should prohibition be repealed, suggesting that drug abuse is more than a straightforward social problem requiring conventional responses, but possesses the ability to change and damage the very nature of society. He expresses genuine fears about something greater than within the realms of current understanding, and would if true, offer a frightening prospect about the future, were any government unwise enough to abandon its current policies. The centrepiece of these fears lies in the selective impact on those least able to resist. It also includes a set of moral questions about the damage drug use can do to our major institutions, to the norms and values surrounding those institutions, to the work ethic surrounding industrial production and to democracy itself (*Hansard*, 1971).

How realistic are these fears? To some extent the answer depends on the current and future size of the problem. A distinction would, I suspect, be drawn by Lord Windelsham between that effecting a small number, and that which reaches epidemic proportions. If seen this way it would be classically utilitarian, that is, about controlling action. Utilitarian thinking is about controls, which should increase according to the extent and severity of the problem, aimed at matching an increase in its size. So, that which concerns only a small number, and where matters are confined primarily to questions about management, the solution is minimum control – probably doing very little, lest intervention might make things worse. An increase in the size of the drug-using population means an increase in the severity of the control. This was how the drug problem was handled in Britain in the 1930s, with a small number of opium addicts, mostly of Chinese origin, living in or around large seaports such as London, Glasgow or Liverpool, plus a number who were therapeutic addicts, that is, addicted having received drugs such as opiates for a terminal condition, some in the medical and allied professions, and a few who had acquired their addiction as a result of recreational use. Controls were minimal. They were 'managed' in the sense that they were prescribed heroin, but mostly they were left alone, lest to do otherwise might draw attention to their plight and thereby exacerbate it. The explanation of their drug use was tailored to fit the size of the problem; who could blame the Chinese, when 'chasing the dragon' was part of their culture, or the therapeutic addict who deserved sympathy rather than condemnation having been prescribed heroin to meet a terminal condition. If the remainder was made up of the foolish and the renegade, then so be it: none was a threat to the social or moral order. When the numbers of heroin addicts increased, the policy changed (Bean, 1974; Spear, 2002).

Nowadays, the drug problem is extensive, and in utilitarian terms requires additional appropriate controls. It is not simply its size and extent, for that is bad enough given that the UK has the largest numbers of drug users in Western Europe, it is also what the users represent. Many modern drug users come from working-class offender populations, or at least those who represent the greatest social threat – it is estimated that in 2005 there were 300,000 problem 'hard core' drug users who were responsible for a multitude of social problems. To be swamped with large numbers of these drug users is to the prohibitionist a fearful prospect. There is also a serious point to consider about the impact of legalisation falling disproportionately on members of the underclass. Note that, Inciardi and McBride (1991, p 65) talk about legalisation as 'serving to legitimate the chemical destruction of an urban generation and culture'. They call it a programme of social management and control that would further damage an already fragile social fabric of the ghetto. Certainly it is a world where serial stepfatherhood has replaced fatherhood, or more likely there is no male presence in the home, and where gang control has replaced family and social ties. It is in this atmosphere that drug abuse flourishes. Inciardi and McBride are correct to puncture the hope that these problems will somehow disappear if drugs are legalised. The hope is a fond one but hardly realistic, for although prohibition may have made a bad situation worse, it did not create it, nor will it be solved by its departure. The epidemiological evidence suggests that drug abuse has remained stubbornly active within working-class deprived housing estates, especially where there are large numbers of people from minority ethnic groups. It is these people who Inciardi and McBride say will bear the brunt of legalisation.

Ultimately the debate is about the moral visions of society, with the prohibitionists fearing for the future should the rules be relaxed, and the legalisers offering what Inciardi and McBride (1991, pp 70, 72) call the remarkable surety of belief in the elixir of legalisation, and the further chemicalisation of the inner cities. As part of this moral vision, the UK government produced a series of strategies in which a key aim is to 'empower individuals and communities, and regenerate neighbourhoods (HM Government, 2002). It sets out these again in 2007 and in 2008 (HM Government, 2007, 2008) in its Consultation Paper and Action Plan, under the heading 'Protecting families and communities'. They extend some of the earlier strategies including 'Engaging and empowering communities', this time suggesting stronger law enforcement, directed at reducing the supply of drugs. There was also a new package for families, which encourages drug-abusing parents to have access to treatment, giving support to carers who will take responsibility for substance-abusing parents, and strengthening the role of schools. It is not the aim here to evaluate these strategies, but show how the government, as a prohibitionist, emphasises the importance of strengthening community ties, although one wonders what terms like 'Engaging and empowering communities' really mean. Even so, the recognition that drug abuse damages more than the individual is clearly high on the government's priorities. It means that the government is not, in Lord Windelsham's phrase, 'standing by while a disabling and unnatural habit flourishes' (*Hansard*, 1971).[1]

It is interesting that money laundering is rarely mentioned, yet money laundering can be disruptive whether to economic activity, local financial institutions or the structure of the immediate society. In small, fragile economies, traffickers and launderers have distorted local markets, and while larger economies are better protected the threat is still there. The Matrix Knowledge Group (2007), in their study of drug markets and dealers in the UK, found that a large proportion of drug profits went into the legitimate economy, including 'paying the mortgage' and much too on funding a lavish lifestyle. Nonetheless, legitimate businesses were used to launder the money, with the assistance of corrupt professionals (for example lawyers) to facilitate their activities. It remains a puzzle why prohibitionists and legalisers alike have said so little about its dangers. One would have expected something more specific.

Not surprisingly, the claim from many legalisers of various hues, is that existing problems are a result of prohibition, not the other way round. They add that such problems can only be resolved when prohibition ends. Therefore, they say, to play on fears about future dangers is disingenuous, given that the problems were themselves created by prohibition policies. They would cite, correctly, the US 'war on drugs' as an example where rhetoric and practice has damaged the very institutions it was designed to preserve. The 1988 Anti Drug Abuse Act created new crimes and new penalties where for first-time drug offenders the penalties are beyond comprehension; 5g of cocaine can lead to a prison sentence of between five and 40 years. Those with previous drug convictions can receive a mandatory life sentence. Such severity undermines respect for the penal code, it violates basic principles of just deserts, let alone failing to deal effectively with the drug problem. These long periods of imprisonment are economically and socially expensive, and go beyond any likely damage caused by the drugs themselves. The US is not alone in passing such sentences: the death penalty is available in many countries for traffickers, especially in South East Asia. Legalisers see these harms as greater than those created by drug taking.

Legalisers also point to damage to other major institutions. For example, those who seek the right to use recreational drugs say that in order to protect the few who cannot manage their drug taking, the majority are denied what they see as mainly a self-harming activity. They say that such restrictions on liberty are just as damaging as the use of drugs, where liberties once lost are difficult to regain. The reply from prohibitionists is that drug taking is *sui generis* and not therefore comparable to other social problems, requiring its own special measures and solutions. This of course is a justification for state paternalism at its most extreme whether directed at users or non-users alike.[2]

Legalisers say that not enough attention is paid to the dangers of prohibition. Many US states have public health laws where pregnant drug users can be detained until they give birth – here paternalism affects both mother and child. Paternalism with its nascent conflict with autonomy runs throughout the drug control system, and can be a dangerous concept if left unchecked. These are not fanciful fears. What sort of world would it be for drug users, or the rest of us, if paternalism was practised in an unrestrained form? Levels of insecurity would be raised, knowing that anyone deemed a drug user could be required to receive treatment. We have learned from other situations, especially those dealing with people with mental health problems and people with learning difficulties, that as a general rule the greater the levels of state intervention in people's lives the more trouble it brings. We are not good at doing things to or for people, as the history of public intervention shows. And acting in people's best interests, whether they agree or not, has been even less fruitful. Few would deny that some people need help and may be unwilling to accept it. What matters is how paternalism is practised.

The battle for the soul of society is dominated by the prohibitionists, where they evoke strong fears for the future. Legalisers have tended not to engage in this debate, preferring a more restrained response. Yet in their way their visions are just as prominent, whether through the 'perfect legalisers' of the free marketers or of the legal moralists. The difference is that legalisers rarely talk in these grand terms, but some of their proposals would produce equally intrusive change. The difference between them is that the legalisers' fears are of the present, the prohibitionists' are of the future.

The personal

At the personal level, and to repeat the point, Lord Windelsham again puts matters clearly:

> Drugs are responsible for the undermining of family and community life. The misery drug misuse causes cannot be underestimated. Drug misuse destroys the lives of individuals, families and communities. It destroys potential, and hope, and preys on the most vulnerable young people.... Very often jobs and homes are lost, friendship and family ties are broken. Where children are involved there is a danger of abandonment and neglect. (*Hansard*, 1971)

Inciardi and McBride again, this time on reasons for prohibiting cannabis:

> This research documents what clinicians have been saying for years. Personal growth evolves through learning to cope with stress, anxiety, frustration, and the many other difficulties that life presents, both small and large. Marijuana use (and other drugs as well including alcohol) particularly among adolescents and young adults, interferes with this process, and the result is a drug arrested development. (Inciardi and McBride, 1991, p 51)

Lord Windelsham's fears are appropriate for a number of drug users, but of course not all, and then mainly for that group described above, that is, a specific sub-population from deprived social areas. These sub-populations are of young people with poor social skills, low educational attainment and a delinquent lifestyle (Bean, 2008). The public perception of this group is of a feckless, work shy and criminal group whose drug taking is an extension to their deviant lifestyle. That this is not the whole picture is neither here nor there, but public perception accounts for a lot. Data from the 2003 Crime and Justice Survey (Becker and Roe, 2005) show that 16% of those defined as 'vulnerable' reported to have used Class A drugs in the previous year, whereas the reported use of Class A drugs in the previous year was markedly low among young people in the general population (4%). Among the identified groups, truants had the highest levels of drug use (16%). It is not uncommon to see young people aged 25 who have taken drugs for 10 years or more and never had a job. 'Rehabilitation' is not an option; 'habilitation' is the only possibility.

The same dismal picture emerges with regard to their economic well-being. In my study of prostitutes (Bean, in preparation) many said that they earned 'funny money' – occasionally £300 – per night but were often homeless, poorly fed, badly clothed and impoverished in almost every economic sense. If they earned £300 per night then they spent £300 per night on drugs. On that basis one would expect their immediate dealers to be wealthy, but like their customers, that was rarely so. A small number of senior dealers, usually from outside the local geographical area, do well, but they do not use the product, and take all profits out of the geographical area in which the drugs are sold. For those remaining, the result is a downward spiral in the drug using/dealing cycle.

What we know from studies of the health of current users is that nearly two thirds (64%) report physical health issues and 50% mental health issues in addition to drug misuse (see Bean, 2006). Small-scale surveys on drug users living on the streets, usually begging (or 'panhandling' to use the American terminology) report even higher rates (Bean, 2006). They show that users have severe health problems and a poor prognosis. Over the years their major organs have suffered and their immune systems are damaged. If they inject, and almost all street drug users do, they are at risk from HIV/AIDS, or hepatitis C. Irrespective of the types of drugs taken, the extent of use or whether use is from prescribed drugs, including heroin or methadone, the risk always remains that users may suffer from a range of health problems such as respiratory irregularities or dental hygiene – methadone, for example, has high sugar levels, which damage teeth – or excessive weight loss, muscle wasting, alongside other diseases related to a chaotic lifestyle and poor and erratic nutrition.

Women face the same health problems as men. They share the same risks and dangers from similar chaotic lifestyles, except that some women face greater risks; for example, the lifestyle associated with crack/cocaine use often includes physical abuse and outright violence. Medical complications go undetected and untreated, especially among prostitutes who with a history of sexually transmitted diseases are at a high risk of cervical cancer (Inciardi et al, 1993, p 142). Pregnant women not only have their own health problems but risk transferring them to the unborn child. Maternal drug abuse may affect the child at every stage of its development: the utero-ovarian environment may not be optimal, the neonatal period may be complicated by a drug withdrawal syndrome, and if substance abuse continues the child's physical and emotional development may be adversely affected by growing up in a drug-taking environment.

These examples suggest that personal problems associated with drug abuse are real, urgent and of considerable concern. The fear is that they may be made worse. Prohibitionists have always claimed that while their policies are not ideal, they represent the best of a bad lot, a sort of 'devil you know' type argument. Take, for example, the health problems described above. Prohibitionists say that it cannot be assumed that these health risks will disappear if drugs are made legal. However, assume some do. Assume that users are more knowledgeable about public health matters than before, and there is a reduction in health problems. This of course would produce an important advance and a net benefit for the legalisers. But can we take that chance? Might an increase in use produce a corresponding increase in health risks? Prohibitionists always assert that to take that chance would produce long-lasting, serious health problems, without parallel in our history. However, to claim a bad situation could be made worse is not a sound reason for remaining with the status quo.

Some legalisers are prepared to take that chance, believing that it is no business of the state to protect families, heal fractured relationships or save everyone from the hundred and one other things to which flesh is heir. The responsibility is not that of the state but of the individual. Others believe that as a result of their proposals many of the problems will fade away, prohibition having been the original cause.

Unfortunately, for most drug users, one suspects that this debate means little. They live their lives much as the rest of us, and come to no harm as a result of the drugs. In this sense they would not be greatly affected were legalisation to occur, except of course they would no longer be committing an offence. The 'clubber' taking cannabis or ecstasy on a Saturday night may well be holding down a regular job, as may the intermittent smoker of cocaine and the occasional user of heroin. Of course the prohibitionists say that occasional use often leads to persistent use. (In a research study in Nottingham in 1994 we found a small number of young professionals, businesspeople and so on taking extensive quantities of crack. Two years later they were nowhere to be seen! Whether they had stopped using cocaine, moved away or something dire had happened we were unable to say. We were unable to find them (Bean and Wilkinson, 1988). Estimates vary about the numbers of occasional users who succumb, and vary according to the drug, but the guess would be about 75% of heroin users, and 10% of crack users, with probably no more than 5% for ecstasy. But these are guesses, nothing more. An implication of these figures is that prohibition denies the right of many to use drugs in order to restrict and restrain the actions of the few who will be a danger to themselves and society's future. The number of people who are perceived to be in danger varies according to what they take and how often they take it, but as I say, most come to no harm. Drug abuse has to be seen in this perspective, and I say this without denying that there is a sub-population of users who are a danger to themselves and others.

Commercial systems

At a less abstract level, what sort of commercial systems would be needed to meet the demands of the legalisers? All the proposals listed in Chapters Two and Three include suggestions about the way drugs are to be distributed and supplied. Some suggest by medical prescription, others through the market, and within each, and as expected, are various subdivisions.

In an attempt to simplify matters, I want to set the ideal types along a continuum, ranging from increased availability to extensive controls (Kleiman and Saiger, 1990, p 541). The more enthusiastic the legaliser, the more will the drugs be positioned at the available end of the spectrum, but even then things are not straightforward. I recognise that some proposals involve making selected drugs more freely available, while prohibiting others such as heroin or crack/cocaine. And different again are those where prohibition is determined by the status of the users, that is, those which restrict availability to, say, juveniles but offer generous availability for adults. Nonetheless, to simplify matters and speaking generally, the economic libertarians and moral rights theorists are placed at one end of the spectrum, with the decriminalisers, the medicalisers and harm reductionists in the middle, and the prohibitionists at the other end. In practice, things are more complicated, for there is no simple continuum that separates things in that comfortable way.

As far as commercial supply systems are concerned, I think it is possible to detect a number of models, and I want to look at each in turn.

The supermarket model

The first of the models I have called the 'supermarket model'. In this model there is a high level of availability, with few restrictions on consumption, that is, the drugs would be marketed according to standard market regulations, where the weight, potency and price would be labelled, as with other products sold in the store. The drugs would be produced, sold and marketed by commercial enterprises, where companies would aim to increase sales through competition. Drugs such as the opiates and opiate derivatives would be sold in ways similar to products such as codeine. Commercial decisions would be made about the location of the outlets – should they be in poor areas, where there is a concentration of users, or in rich areas, where the sales potential is greater? Or both? Would the supermarket be open 24 hours a day? Would the drugs be sold in specialist stores or through the supermarket chains? Presumably, they might be purchased direct from the producers, as in Colombia or wherever, but that would present no additional complications. Purchasing would be similar to the existing system where legally controlled opiates are purchased, manufactured and distributed through the NHS. All these questions are administrative and matters for the supermarket itself; they are about reducing costs and maximising profits. They are not moral issues to be decided on the basis of individual welfare and community preservation.

The supermarket model could incorporate a limited number of restrictions in the same way as it currently copes with the sale of alcohol and tobacco. Sales might be only by specialist sales personnel along the lines suggested by Transform, that is, with a specialist pharmacist trained and qualified to dispense certain drugs, adhering to certain limited legal regulations and restrictions. The drugs may be on display, or they may not, and in the same way that contemporary supermarket practices vary, so there might be variations in procedures and restrictions, that is, as long as the basic principles remained; drugs would be sold as a commercial enterprise, with few restrictions on sales to adult customers. Of course the supermarket model removes every bulwark created by prohibition against the destructive effects of drug use, and increases the possibility of greater use.

The supermarket model involves traditional supermarket methods of the open display of the product, the development of specialist retail outlets, and door-to-door salespeople perhaps selling their wares alongside other home sales syndicates. Should these be tolerated? Yes, if that is what a supermarket model means. What would be the impact of the various brands of crack/cocaine being advertised in open competition, glorifying the merits of each respective brand, with heroin, crack and the like being sold in specialist outlets? From the salesperson's point of view, it means an increase in sales and a corresponding increase in profits.

What to do about advertising? If permitted, what might we expect of the advertisements? In the supermarket model there would be no restrictions on advertising, so we might expect the new Marlborough Man to be smoking crack instead of cigarettes, and overworked truck drivers alongside tired executives reaching for their evening pick-me-up of cocaine. Heroin could be portrayed as a way to relax after a tiring day (Inciardi and McBride, 1991, p 57). Or, it might follow the current practice for alcohol and tobacco and be more subtle, rarely providing a description of what the drug actually does. It could be associational, by promoting hopes of sex and glamour should a particular product be taken, or associating the product with sporting events and thereby sporting prowess. Inciardi and McBride say that these are not fanciful speculations; the aim of all advertising is to market the product and increase demand. Advertising becomes one of the most powerful tools of modern capitalism, being the vehicle by which the ability of an entrepreneurial system is able to create, expand and maintain high levels of demand (Inciardi and McBride, 1989, p 270). And if, as a result, there is an increase in use then so be it. The old maxim remains: 'If it is legal to sell a product then it should be legal to advertise it.'

Friedman's (Friedman and Szasz, 1992) commercial model for drugs would fit the supermarket model but with some restrictions on advertising. Stevenson, however, wants to ban advertising, in fact he wants drugs to bear a government health warning – his model leans more towards the mail order model described below (Stevenson, 1994, p 66). Legal moralists such as Husak support the supermarket model by default, that is, they want the right to use drugs, therefore it is reasonable to assume they want the right for drugs to be sold openly. Yet, surprisingly, they react against advertising. They believe that it should be banned, if only to show sceptics that legal moralists are serious about preventing any increase in use (Husak, 1992, p 225). This of course neatly slides over some of the implications of their position, showing a penchant for sitting on the fence when things get difficult. Husak says that the rights of the drug users are not violated by a ban on advertising. The advertisers are the ones who suffer – 'smokers had no cause for complaint when greater restrictions were imposed on the advertising of tobacco' (Husak, 1992, p 225). He admits that the 'waters are muddy' and he 'can do little to clarify them' (1992, p 225). If the right to use a substance also produces the right to purchase it then Husak is correct to say this must extend to a right to sell it (Husak 1992). If so, a ban violates those rights. He, like Stevenson, wants it both ways, for the only reason to ban advertising is a fear about a likely increase in use.

What about tax? This is another dilemma for legalisers. If it is too high then the illegal market will flourish and be able to undercut a legally commercial system, albeit by an inferior contaminated product. If it is too low, the black market will be weakened, but revenue will be reduced. So old-fashioned utilitarian considerations must be applied: at what point are taxes sufficiently high to generate revenue, but low enough to destroy illegal markets (Husak, 1992, p 227)? That the products will be taxed is a certainty, optimistically stated by one legaliser as providing revenue for the treatment of addicted users, but more likely being nothing more than a general revenue-producing activity. If, however, taxation is to be used in a similar way to taxes on alcohol and tobacco, that is, as a way of discouraging use, then this is something else again. As always, John Stuart Mill got to the heart of the matter when he said: 'to tax stimulants for the sole purpose of making them more difficult to obtain is a measure differing only in degree from their entire prohibition, and would be justifiable only if that were justified' (quoted in Husak, 1992, p 228). Generally speaking, legalisers believe that drugs should be taxed as for any other commodity. Not for them the agony of debating whether taxes encourage or discourage use; that is a matter for individuals and parents, not for governments.

What the supermarket model does is show how full-scale legalisation might work. It produces few restrictions and few regulations, the emphasis being on the ease and certainty of distribution and supply. Its strengths and weaknesses are apparent. One obvious weakness is shown by the problems already created by the sale of over-the-counter painkillers, and gives succour to the fears that the greater level of availability will result in a greater level of use. The point was made in a House of Lords debate (House of Lords, 22 January 2009, col 1778, *Hansard*) that addiction to these substances is becoming a serious problem. There are more than 30,000 people who may depend on drugs containing codeine, with middle-aged women most at risk. Some are taking more than 70 pills a day, putting themselves in danger of liver dysfunction, stomach disorders, gallstones, constipation and depression (House of Lords, 22 January 2009, col 1778, *Hansard*). Apparently the internet was making it easier for people to buy bulk supplies of drugs, including Solpadeine and Nurofen Plus. The conclusion in the House of Lords debate was that restricting the availability of codeine was very important (House of Lords, 22 January 2009, col 1778, *Hansard*). It did not say how, but the UK government (through the National Institute for Health and Clinical Excellence) could require manufacturers to reduce particular constituents, in the same way governments could insist that manufacturers reduce the alcohol content of beer and wine. The abuse of over-the-counter drugs containing narcotic and/or psychotropic substances is an increasing problem. They are drugs of first choice for many, and while they may not contain large amounts of addictive substances, if taken in large-enough quantities, the 'high' they produce is comparable to an illicitly manufactured drug.

The right of access model or mail order model

Nadelmann (1991) says that this model operates in ways where customers order the drugs, but unlike the supermarket model, do not receive them immediately. The delay is to act as a cooling-off period, avoiding impulsive and ill-considered buying. It is based on the notion that adults have the right to possess drugs for personal consumption, and obtain them from reliable legally regulated sources, which are responsible and liable for their products. Karel (1991, pp 82-7) opts for a similar version, calling it the bank teller system, whereby a bank card would be used to restrict and regulate use, thereby limiting purchase over a selected period. The bank teller system would be used for cocaine and opium and the opiates. The aim, as with the mail order model, is to frustrate excessive demand.

This mail order model is said to strike at the heart of what is wrong with prohibition, as it retains in skeletal form the essence of a legalised regime with the power to deny access. It allows harm reduction programmes to be imposed on it, and it addresses some of the tensions between individuals and the community by removing some of the worst aspects of illegal markets (Nadelmann, 1991). But of course it does not eliminate illegal markets, which could continue to supply drugs to juveniles (there would be restrictions on the supply to those under a certain age) and some users might want to circumvent the waiting period. And of course as soon as any model moves away from direct availability towards a form of prohibition, legal and moral decisions appear. These are about the drugs to be controlled, and the appropriate sanctions for those breaking the rules. Nor does it meet the fear of an increase in use, which, to his credit, Nadelmann addresses. He says that the mail order model might actually encourage existing users to engage in more destructive behaviour, whether through the use of different drugs or through greater use of existing ones. He also suspects that a heightened level of tolerance would lead to greater levels of experimentation, and encourage new users – underlining a point made by critics when cannabis was reclassified in Britain from a Class B drug to a Class C drug.

Advertising within the mail order model would be similar to that in the supermarket model. The mail order model is not aimed at reducing use, more at reducing impulsive use, although it is suspected that the more aggressive forms of advertising might be actively discouraged if not banned. Taxation would be as in the supermarket model.

The gatekeeping model

The third model – the gatekeeping model – moves further towards prohibition, bringing with it a corresponding increase in moral problems. Again, as with the other models, this one can incorporate a range of restrictions, and requires moral decisions about the drugs selected for control. Gatekeeping would appear to be the favoured model of the medicalisers, who emphasise the importance of regulated markets. This model has physicians and pharmacists intervening between seller and consumer, where the gatekeepers decide who will receive and provide the drugs, the amounts provided and the conditions under which they are taken. The police, as additional gatekeepers, will prosecute those who violate the rules; possession is by consent of the gatekeepers. In this model, customer choice has been weakened, but customers still have access to the gatekeepers, and generally speaking can apply for the drugs of choice and expect to have them provided. Some gatekeepers may require additional conditions to be fulfilled before the drugs are delivered, others may be more flexible. Not all drugs will be controlled by gatekeepers – I suggest those mainly designated as Class A, and perhaps a few in Class B under the 1971 Misuse of Drugs Act. Others could be sold according to the supermarket model, others again according to the mail order model depending on choice or preference. What separates this model from the two above is that customer choice is more restricted, and sanctions are more robust.

In the gatekeeping model, the level of availability decreases, but the controls increase. As most drugs would be provided by medical gatekeepers they will presumably be on prescription, or in Karel's (1991, p 88) words 'the authority of physicians to prescribe drugs as they see fit would be restored'. In the UK, the supply and distribution would presumably be through the NHS. But not entirely: there might be private prescriptions, as there are now. The decision to prescribe and amounts to be prescribed would not be the decision of the users (patients) but a clinical decision by the physician/gatekeeper. A number of other substances, not controlled through the gatekeepers, perhaps cannabis, might be available through other commercial outlets. The resulting commercial system would be a mixture of distribution outlets, some through government-controlled centres, some through the supermarket model, some similar to those currently controlled by the pharmacy and poisons legislation, but the most harmful would be through medical prescribing. The Transform Drug Policy Foundation offers a range of procedures by which the drugs would be distributed. At the top they would be distributed through medical prescription (that is, the most harmful drugs through gatekeepers), then through the licensed premises such as coffee shops and finally there would be the over-the-supermarket-counter sales, which presumably would be under the same auspices as patent medicines controlled under the various medicines legislation.

In effect, the gatekeeping model allows the gatekeeper to select the drugs and control them through policies that are backed by criminal laws involving sanctions. The coffee shops of Holland provide a rough equivalent of a modern gatekeeping model where specified limited quantities of cannabis are purchased from licensed owners, except that the drug would need to be labelled according to strength and content. The drawbacks are clear: the gatekeeper model raises again the spectre of illegal markets. That is to say, the more extensive the restrictions the more opportunities there are for illegal markets to flourish, for in spite of what is said, the gatekeeping model will produce restrictions that some users might be unwilling or unlikely to accept. The other difficulty is that crack/cocaine may not be included. That, as said above, will promote illegal markets and in doing so move the whole model further towards prohibition.

The gatekeeping model has not always met with success. It is strange that modern gatekeepers have ignored the possibility that gatekeeping may produce its own set of problems as a result of overprescribing or less than careful prescribing. I do not want to raise again the spectre of overprescribing in the 1960s but I do want to point to a more contemporary situation, that is, the large numbers of what used to be called 'therapeutic addicts', who are addicted to prescription drugs such as valium, including some such as morphine controlled by the 1971 Misuse of Drugs Act. Yet, 'The abuse and trafficking of prescription drugs is set to exceed illicit drug abuse' so warned the International Narcotics Control Board (INCB) in its *Annual Report* (INCB, 2008, press release, p 1). Typical abusers in the UK are the large numbers of 'therapeutic addicts' on many general practitioner (GP) caseloads. These are patients who may have originally been prescribed painkillers such as the benzodiazepines for personal problems (sleeplessness) or arthritis, or after an accident, or even that group of patients whose medical condition is their life's work. Most GPs will have about 10 to 15 such patients on their caseload who over a period of time are taking huge quantities of painkillers. Prescribing is often out of control; the patient's behaviour descends into a drug-seeking activity where they over-report symptoms in order to obtain a larger prescription (Bean and Ravenscroft, 2004). Most such patients have been on prescriptions for years.

These examples offer a warning, if only to show how legally regulated markets do not always provide the expected solutions. The problems of over-the-counter medicines and the 'therapeutic addicts' are stubborn reminders that solutions are complex. We struggle to cope with the alcohol problem, but at least accept that a problem exists; those of the over-the-counter sales or the 'therapeutic addicts' remain largely unrecognised yet with a potential to be serious.

Within the gatekeeping model there is general agreement that advertising should be banned, backed in some cases with prominent displays of legitimate health warnings. McVay (1992, p 153), another medicaliser, also wants a ban on advertising and the introduction of mechanisms that regulate cannabis production. Karel (1991, p 94) says that advertising would be prohibited, but then talks of 'word of mouth' advertising. That means the consumer would have to learn through government authority or through friends, relatives or official bulletins where the substances are dispensed. The less harmful substances could be advertised in the same way as coffee or tea. Public consumption would not be permitted. Other medicalisers such as Transform are opposed to advertising, this being one of a number of 'activities that would remain prohibited', others being consumption in public places and unlicensed sales (Transform, 2007, p 33).

In this I detect a whiff of hypocrisy. Thornton as a perfect legaliser is at least consistent, believing that a market philosophy involves accepting certain parameters, and that includes advertising. But to offer a semi-market model, which is what gatekeeping is, where certain drugs are available, but not allowed to be advertised, is to hide behind the fear that what is being offered is dangerous and must be reigned in. A more honest approach would be to publicly acknowledge possible dangers. If legalisers are sufficiently confident in their proposals then they should openly admit their strengths and weaknesses. If they do not then we are left with the suspicion that the future is more uncertain than they would have us believe, and their proposals are on less than firm foundations.

Taxation presents further difficulties. Transform (2007) does not say what its taxation policy would be except that it wants legal companies to pay tax, that is, those supplying the drugs, and be subject to external scrutiny as well as answerable to the law. It sees 'profit margins as 100% or more' for those companies so it concludes that there is 'plenty of room for manoeuvre for policy makers regarding tax and price control' (Transform, 2006, p 26). It says that 'even with taxes legally supplied drugs would still dramatically undercut illicit markets' (Transform, 2007, p 33). McVay (1992, p 153) wants 'a pricing structure that discourages consumption while denying criminals market supremacy'. Taxes, he says, must be economically viable, but low enough so as not to create strong incentives for a black market. He is right. High taxation may make drugs so expensive that in practical terms they are out of reach to potential customers. Legal availability does not connote with easy availability (Nadelmann, 1991).

Karel continues to offer ingenious if not wholly convincing solutions to the various problems. He wants to use taxation as a means of denying criminals market supremacy. He says: 'Addicts would be provided drugs on their ability to pay. They would never be forced to resort to crime to support a habit' (Karel, 1991, p 94). That means undertaking a complex financial assessment of the user's means. There are two problems with this. First, I cannot believe many physicians will be sufficiently determined to undertake a full financial assessment of a drug user, and decide on the addict's ability to pay. Second, how much to charge and what if the user challenges the decision or finds other reasons not to pay? And the price must be sufficiently low to undercut the cost from the illegal markets, otherwise their supremacy will be retained.

Incidentally, I have said little about harm reduction and decriminalisation largely because they have had little to say about the commercial nature of drug supply and distribution. Advertising and taxation are not within their remit, nor is the supply and distribution of drugs through commercial outlets. Traditionally, they have not been greatly concerned with the commercial features of legalisation, although of course all programmes aimed at reducing use, whether through taxation or otherwise, can be said to reduce harms, and all concerned with sanctions in whatever form are the province of decriminalisation.

Varied and traditional prohibition

The fourth model closely resembles traditional prohibition where the law regulates the production, distribution and consumption of selected substances. Of course prohibition is much more complicated than that, and it would be more appropriate to divide it into a number of models. But for these purposes a single model will do. Under all forms of prohibition, some drugs will be available in supermarkets (codeine and the like) and some through prescription by gatekeepers. What distinguishes prohibition from all other models is there is no opportunity to choose certain restricted drugs, purchase them or consume them without authority. Prohibition provides the greatest measure of control, sometimes with severe sanctions.

There is no need to describe in detail the key features of prohibition, as these are implicit throughout. There is a need, however, to emphasise some of the lessons that prohibition provides, which seem to be lost on some of the legalisers. Prohibition emphasises the importance drugs pose as a threat to the future of society, it plays upon fears about the addictive quality of certain drugs, and the surrounding lifestyle of the users. Above all, it fosters claims that drug taking is *sui generis* and destructive. Implied in much of what prohibitionists say and do is classical utilitarianism, whereby social problems take on a different hue when they become extensive. Unchecked and uncontrolled health problems, high levels of unemployment accompanied by what is already described as urban blight, would, say the prohibitionists, pose long-term problems, which may take generations to remove. They would say that these fears cannot be replaced by sleight of hand or dismissed easily, or by the unjustified optimism that every thing will be alright if we could only replace prohibition with this or that model or this or that new proposal. We need something more concrete than that.

Clearly, some prohibitionists have exaggerated their case and have not always acted wisely. Take, for example, the way prohibitionists constantly talk of 'drugs' in that generic form without any consideration of their different impact. Nadelmann (1991, pp 38-40) is almost alone in drawing attention to this. He says that no one denies that heroin and cocaine are dangerous but with respect to the hallucinogens such as LSD and cannabis their potential for addiction is virtually nil. He believes we should examine the impact of each drug, and then decide on ways it should be marketed, perhaps concluding with a market system similar to that of alcohol or tobacco, that is, to regard them as being consumed by many who come to no harm, but by a few who become addicted and harm themselves or others as a consequence. This would presumably take some of the heat and fervour out of the debate, and place the likelihood of a cataclysmic future in greater perspective. On the other hand, some legalisers have also damaged their case with hyperbolic and fanciful claims promoting unrealistic expectations. These undermine their position and induce scepticism. Their failure is they do not extend the same degree of self-criticism as they give to others. Take, for example, the accusation by some legalisers that drug laws are unenforceable. They might be, but to ignore that possibility when it applies to their own proposed regulations makes it difficult to believe they understand the implications of what they are saying. Or that their proposed market system offers a solution, without including the possibility of failure.

The internet

I have said nothing about the increasing role of the internet in the marketing, supply and distribution of illegal and unauthorised prescription drugs.Yet this model is of considerable significance already, and likely to have a greater impact in the future. Recommendation 44 of the INCB report for 2007 (INCB, 2008, paras 250-8) states that the misuse of the internet and postal and courier services has become an escalating problem (para 250). It describes the extent of internet use, whether for illegal or prescription drugs (2008, paras 250-8) and says that it is 'alarmed by the continuing rise of Internet sales' (para 250) – for example in the US in 2006 there were 34 illegal internet pharmacies, which dispensed with more than 98 million dosage units of hydrocone products. Most internet sites were in the US but the country with the next largest number was the UK (paras 250/251) (see also *The Guardian*, 19 February, 2009).

The INCB is right to be alarmed given the potential of the internet to dominate the supply and distribution of drugs, the latter through courier services. Such are the opportunities for expansion it could dwarf all other supply networks. Its weaknesses lie in the distribution services, where the use of couriers leads to uncertain results, as increasing surveillance techniques allow packages to be intercepted and the receivers prosecuted. Suppliers are more difficult to identify: they use encryption messages and are able to hide the source of their internet services. Nonetheless, the INCB paints a gloomy picture with new trafficking routes opening regularly. The outcome is uncertain, but likely that the type of supply models listed above will become less important when the internet offers supplies with considerably less risk and more ease, one way being for traffickers to have their own distribution/courier services. The Guardian suggests an INCB 'Coordinated global response is needed to meet the challenge' (*The Guardian*, 19 February 2009).

A digression: the sale of alcohol

There is considerable literature on promoting the sale of products such as alcohol. It is part of the muddle we get ourselves into that these products are legal but harmful, whereas others are illegal but less harmful. We have to accept that muddle. The alcohol and tobacco industries remain powerful and comparatively respectable, with a host of respectable shareholders. They have been able to stay apart and avoid the infamous reputations of those manufacturing and selling drugs. At present, the control and supply of alcohol raises questions about how to reach a balance between acceptable and unacceptable levels of use – for these purposes I avoid defining 'acceptability'. We can usefully ask: what can be learned from models derived from the modern-day sales and distribution of alcohol, which could be used in the sales and distribution of drugs?

Take, for example, the 'integration model'. This model uses the strength of social customs to modify and restrict drinking habits. The integration model has a commonsense appeal but only where cultures can exert a degree of discipline over their members, particularly the adolescents. Some clearly cannot; witness the binge drinking on the streets of our cities at weekends or the way alcohol has decimated the cultures of indigenous American and Australasian peoples. Integration means a mixture of the traditional carrot and stick, encouragement and disapproval, encouraging children to drink responsibly when they are young and expressing disapproval when they do not, all in the hope that it will encourage greater regulation in later life. It is difficult to see how such practices can be manipulated into a workable policy in the light of contemporary lifestyles. And of course it means offsetting those lifestyles against something deep within Anglo-Saxon culture that sees heavy drinking and drunkenness as linked to enjoyment and a good night out. Restraint for this group is rarely an option. The other problem is that, unlike other forms of drug use, the aim for most governments is to see alcohol as a source of revenue. Integration not abstinence is their aim (Bakalar and Grinspoon, 1984, pp 100-1).

The integration model has had only limited success. Countries such as France seem to operate it reasonably well in the way young children are acquainted with alcohol, but France still has a high level of adult alcoholism. Some Inuit communities in Canada have successfully applied the integration model, but that has meant living apart and in remote areas, cutting themselves off from other communities, and sometimes banning alcohol altogether. In such communities, where they are successful, there must be a consensus about the norms regulating alcohol use and an agreement about punishments when norms are violated. That level of agreement is unheard of in modern complex societies.

If not the integration model then what of the 'consumption model'? This model involves restricting the supply of alcohol through taxation pricing and licensing. The key feature is to accept that the range of consumption of alcohol is fixed. That means consumption approximates to a normal distribution with some people drinking nothing, and others drinking much more, up to and occasionally beyond the levels of tolerance. The key variable is the statistical mean, which is the peak of the normal distribution. So, if the mean is reduced, and this can be achieved by restricting hours of sale, or through increased taxation, then consumption will be reduced and so will associated problems such as alcoholism, fewer drink-driving accidents and so on (Bakalar and Grinspoon, 1984, pp 102-4). This model is widely recognised and occasionally operated by governments, and with some success. I am not sure that a similar success can be achieved with drugs. If the price of heroin increases, or supply is restricted, users do not give up, unless the price increases hugely. Nonetheless, there is a degree of elasticity of demand so the amount consumed will be affected by a change in price. That means a measure of success, but the impact is likely to be small. More likely users will find a substitute drug or drugs, which produce(s) a similar effect, or in some cases an entirely different effect, and wait until the price drops or stay with the substitute. That is not what happens with alcohol, and these differences impose limitations in transferring such a model across the drugs boundaries.

It is doubtful whether we can learn much from an examination of alcohol controls – the social and economic differences are too great, and the gulf too wide. Comparisons with alcohol suffer because of the social acceptance of alcohol compared with drugs, although the way we have failed to control alcohol consumption ought to act as a warning. There is, however, a certain irony about basing drug policy on an alcohol model when there is increasing concern about levels of alcohol consumption especially among the young and the 'yob' culture created by binge drinking. And, for that matter, an irony too about legalising cannabis when more restrictions are imposed on tobacco smoking in the belief that increased controls will produce less consumption.

Notes

[1] The theme is continued in the government's Drug Action Plan (2007) (HM Government, 2008) for 2008-18 where it states that its drug strategy comprises four strands of work: protecting communities through tackling drug supply, drug-related crime and anti-social behaviour; preventing harm to children, young people and families affected by drug misuse; delivering new approaches to drug treatment and social reintegration; and public information campaigns, communications and community engagement.

[2] Paternalism in the form used here is close to *parens patriae*, that is, literally the state as father of the people, where it is the duty of the state to look after those who are unable to look after themselves. An early manifestation of *parens patriae* in English law was the recognition by Edward II in the 14th century of the Sovereign's responsibility towards the property, and later the person of the insane. A modern example, albeit in a slightly different context, can be found under the 1948

National Assistance Act whereby some older people can be removed from their home when they cannot care for themselves. Under *parens patriae*, certification has been regarded as a privilege that brings benefits. As the state has a duty of care, so its agents have a duty to see that care is offered in the circumstances appropriate to the person's needs. In its purist form there is no interest in the aetiology of the condition; its effects are the important determinants.

7

Some concluding thoughts

In the previous chapters a number of proposals for legalising drugs were examined with special reference to crime, the position of juveniles and commercial considerations. The topics discussed include most of the main points in the legalisers' proposals. Arising from this are five questions, which I suggest must be asked if we are to produce a rational drug policy. They involve: the justifications for controlling drugs; the likely implications as far as crime is concerned; commercial considerations; the groups of persons, if any, to be separated to receive special attention; and the type of enforcement that should operate to control rule breakers. Before looking at these I want to give a brief overview of some of the conclusions arising from the ideal types presented in Chapter One.

A general point to make is that within those ideal types discussed, all have limitations, and none, including prohibition, is entirely satisfactory. Beginning with prohibition: it is said to have majority support, yet this is only a partial riposte against criticism, and a device used by governments when it suits them. Its supporters could point to the many exaggerations of the legalisers, or the way they avoid the more difficult features of their proposals. An example can be given from Stevenson (1994, p 14) who says that 'If some people insist on using drugs it is better that they should buy them from law abiding businessmen than from criminals and better still if they can be integrated into society and brought under medical supervision if needed.' The trick here, say Reuter et al (1994, p 86) is in the word 'some'. 'Some' might turn out to be a lot. And even if harms per user are reduced, the total harm created by an increase might be greater.

Prohibition may have its faults, but is not without its virtues. A major virtue, at least of the form of prohibition practised in the

UK, is that it is a jumble of inconsistencies, which paradoxically have the merit of allowing various strands to be developed, and work undertaken within current practices. There may not be a clear or straightforward set of policies, but that is no bad thing. The drug world is too complicated for one approach to dominate. Under prohibition we can prescribe, we can decriminalise, we can legalise and we can promote harm reduction. The trick is to get the correct balance between the various options. There will always be a debate about that. Of course, if prohibition does not stand up to scrutiny, we should amend it. In doing so we need more than the sort of hopeful spirit engendered by Arnold Trebach. It will be remembered that he said of legalisation 'Just do it. Let the pieces fall as they will' (Trebach and Inciardi, 1993, p 80). I am not sure this is sound advice, and in the light of what was said above it appears particularly adventurous. This is not a game where we shake the pieces and sit back and see what happens. To change policy in this uncertain way could be a recipe for disaster, and no responsible government ought to consider it.

Taking an overview of the proposals it is striking how varied they are. Yet in some ways they are similar, especially in their optimism and the belief that crime and the prison population, together with many social and economic problems, will fall away once their proposals are accepted. Claims that their particular version of legalisation will solve all, or nearly all, the problems consistently fail to acknowledge the complexity of the subject matter. Similarly, the belief that changes in the ways that drugs are supplied will lead to criminal organisations being dismantled shows a lack of understanding of those organisations. Illegal markets may respond to legalisation in at least four possible ways, only one of which is to pack up and go away. They can either stay in business illegally, or move into other criminal activities such as illegally importing cars, or become legal and move into legal markets. Of course, the last of these would be to the approval of everyone but that is not the point. There is no possibility of knowing which option will be taken, by which organisations and for how long.

Too often, legalisers have left important assumptions unacknowledged, as with the paternalistic role of the medical profession, or simply ignore some of the consequences of their proposals, such as the possibility that legalisation will promote an increase in use. Not entirely though: Ethan Nadelmann is an exception. At the risk of being repetitive, and by way of emphasis, consider two examples. In the first we must accept Husak's warning about deluding ourselves if we believe we can avoid waging a limited war on behalf of adolescents. With the exception of the perfect legalisers, all want to prohibit the sale and distribution of currently illegal drugs to juveniles, while making them available to adults. The legal, social and commercial confusion this will create is obvious, alongside the immediate and long-term health problems. And where will these errant juveniles obtain their drugs, as some surely will? The answer can only be from an illegal supply system. Thornton is correct; whenever there are controls there is bootlegging and with bootlegging there is crime, in this case juvenile crime. And what to do with those juveniles when they are arrested? The answers remain unclear, but likely not very different from those under prohibition. It means all, or almost all, proposals about juveniles contain a control system, hidden, disguised or overt, which if implemented might be as excessive as that under prohibition, and likely to produce similar results. Only the perfect legalisers avoid such criticisms, yet in doing so they leave themselves open to the accusation of irresponsibility.

In the second, what to do about crack/cocaine? Most have fudged the issue, those who have not have either wanted it banned, in which case we are again back to prohibition, or wanted it legalised or prescribed, in which case there are other objections. If banned, profits from illegal markets continue, if legalised, one question is: what sort of a system is this that allows the ultimate recreational drug to be available on prescription, with no medical justification, when other drugs on the NHS are not prescribed because they are too expensive. And if legalised, there must be the fear of an increase in use. Of course, Friedman's (Friedman and Szasz, 1992) point about prohibition producing and promoting crack/cocaine has to be accepted, but having accepted it, what then to do about it? We should not fall into the belief that the solution lies somewhere else for in doing so we may produce a greater problem than before.

Nonetheless, all the legalisers in their way offer something worth considering, and worth including. All can agree that prohibition does not work, but before abandoning it other policies must be shown to work better. Prohibition should not be abandoned because it is ineffective, unless dramatically so, and certainly not until a demonstratively preferable alternative is found (Husak, 1992). We remain a long way from that. There are within the numerous proposals, including prohibition, components sufficient to formulate a rational drug policy, which although not always articulated nonetheless provide the lens through which future prospects can be assessed. It seems reasonable to hope that a more rational policy will develop, and if it were so, I suggest it should include answers to the following questions listed below. I want to look at each in turn.

What are the justifications for the control of specific substances by the law?

Additional complications arise as some controlled drugs are selected by international organisations rather than because they were a national problem. However, for present purposes assume that governments have complete control, then how best to proceed? The organisation Liberty and the legal moralists have made this question central to their proposals. Seeking justifications for state intervention raises questions that admit to no easy answers, but if there is no right to intervene, prohibition falls at the outset, alternatively, if there is such a right then there exists a justification for prohibitive control. The Wootton Committee (Wootton, 1968) grappled with this matter but came to no firm conclusion. Nevertheless, I want to use the example of this Committee as it provides one of the few opportunities to see how this question can be addressed, at least within the British context.

The Wootton Committee followed the legal moralists' line. It said: 'The great majority of the restrictions currently imposed upon an individual's freedom in this country are defended on the grounds that they are necessary for the safety or well-being of others' (Wootton, 1968, para 13). It then became more tentative, saying: 'while we appreciate the force of this argument, it has to be recognized that no hard and fast line can be drawn between actions that are purely self-regarding, and those that involve wider social consequences' (1968, para 15). It then added: 'Much more controversial, however, is the question whether, and if so, how far, it is justifiable for the law to restrict a man's freedom in what is presumed to be his own interest' (1968, para 14). The Committee concluded: 'Every proposal to restrict the freedom of the individual in his own supposed interests must, therefore, be decided on merits, in the light of the probable severity of any damage that he may inflict upon himself, and of the risk that in damaging himself he may also involuntarily be the cause of injury to others' (1968, para 16).

The Committee pointed to a mixture of harm to others and harm to self as a justification yet said little about how much respective harm was needed to justify legal intervention. Presumably more than mere dislike of the substance, or dislike of the subsequent reactions. If through taking drugs, some might say as a result of my actions of such folly, that through my foolishness I lose my job, my home, my friends, my family, is this more than my misfortune? Of course, my actions will inevitably affect others – my employer, family, friends and so on – but have I behaved in ways to make what I have done a criminal offence, providing a justification for the state to intervene? Lord Windelsham (*Hansard*, 1971) believes so. He sees my actions as harming myself, harming others and in the long run damaging the important social institutions of society. The Wootton Committee believed that account must be taken of public attitudes in such a decision, but which and how much weight to be given it did not say.

Traditional liberal values state that the justification for legal intervention is that the behaviour to be controlled, in this case the drugs, must be capable of harming others. A weakened version includes some forms of harms to self. The former would be Husak's position, the latter that of the Wootton Committee. This

Committee wanted to include the probable severity of any damage that a person may inflict on himself with a risk that in doing so he may involuntarily injure others. The version selected will depend on which is seen as morally acceptable and determine the drugs to be controlled.

If the traditional or more stringent version is selected then the following conditions must be satisfied before the drug is controlled.

- That the use of the drug must create serious immediate harms, and/or be capable of producing long-term harms, and there must be a direct link between the drug and the harms.
- That these harms are primarily harms to others, harms to self being only acceptable in exceptional circumstances such as those creating temporary or permanent loss of consciousness or responsibility.
- That all harms be spelled out in detail.
- If harms to the community or society are to be included these must also be severe and spelled out in detail.

If the weaker version is to be used, then greater emphasis is placed on harms to self. So, for example, following the Wootton Committee, drugs such as the opiates or the synthetic opiates would qualify as they are capable of producing harms to self and to others, especially family, to a considerable degree. Given the size of the drug problem, 'public attitudes' might be included, as might the cost of resources and fears for the future of society. Of course, once these are included we move towards a more subjective view where personal judgments begin to intrude and utilitarian considerations dominate.

In the traditional version, the control of certain drugs would be reserved for those meeting the criteria listed above. In practice this would include crack/cocaine, 'ice' (methamphetamine) and perhaps heroin alongside synthetic opiates such as methadone. It might also include LSD. The presumption would be that the drugs to be included would not meet the criteria unless proven otherwise, i.e a negative presumption, rather than the more positive one that they meet the criteria unless proven that they do not.

In the weaker version the same presumption should apply, but with the criteria less strict. That means more drugs would be included. This version might include cannabis if the strength and potency was shown to produce severe long term effects. So too might other amphetamines, but not ecstasy. Nor would most other drugs currently controlled as Class C where the short term and long term effects are minimal, for example certain tranquillisers and ketamine.

So, to the question 'what are the justifications for controlling certain drugs?' the answer must be in terms of the harms caused by the drugs, and according to the stricter or weaker versions offered above. Too often in Britain we have assumed that control is justified where there are minimum harms, i.e. not even meet the demands of the weaker version listed above, as with ketamine or the latest banned substance 'spice' a herbal smoking mixture. This in my view is an unsatisfactory state of affairs where one controlled drug after the other is added for no clear or specific reason but because they are thought to be 'generally harmful.'

Prohibitionists have no difficulty answering a question about harms, presumably relying again on those provided by Lord Windelsham. Yet this justification is somewhat vague, and lacks a certain specificity; 'future dangers' to society ought to be stated, spelled out and where possible listed in order of priority. It is not enough to raise fears; it is necessary to be clear about the nature of those fears, and the conditions in which such fears might arise. Similarly, prohibitionists are concerned about the impact on family life, the loss of self-esteem and so on and these too need to be specified, ideally relating their impact to different drugs. On the other hand, critics of prohibition have done little better; often having failed to take the opportunity to set out their justifications, except by way of decrying prohibition. And herein lies a weakness, not just of prohibition but of legalisers too; for both have failed to be specific and failed to measure up to what should be expected of them. Lord

Windelsham's fears about society's future may be worth stating, but he needs to provide more evidential meat on the bones.

What would be the likely implications as far as crime is concerned?

Prohibition has been blamed for causing large amounts of drug-related crime, with almost all legalisers offering proposals that they say will eliminate this form of criminality. Their optimism is welcome but hardly realistic. Drug-related crime will exist in varying forms and amounts whatever the proposal; it is of course incumbent on those seeking change to lessen that criminality, but equally incumbent on them to show the various links between their proposals and crime. To say, as some have, that illegal markets will disappear is to misunderstand the nature of crime, or the economics of illegal markets, and to fail to consider how adjustments can be made, and how illegal markets can change and develop to fit changing economic circumstances.

What type of enforcement policy should operate to control rule breakers?

Again, all proposals require some forms of enforcement, although rarely has this been included in their portfolio. The belief that drug users only break the rules of prohibition is another of those assumptions rarely considered by most legalisers. It is not just decisions about the type of enforcement but about how much time and resources are to be given to it, and with what expected results. The Wootton Committee (1968, para 18) noted that laws which seek to control the personal consumption of individuals are notoriously hard to enforce. Indeed they are, and many of the problems so created are difficult if not well nigh impossible to solve, or impossible to anticipate. Yet some kinds of dangerous drugs Acts will be required and some enforcement strategies required to deal with the rule breakers.

Following from this, what sanctions should there be for those breaking the laws? How are they to be dealt with? Some suggest that offenders will be fined, but what of those who do not pay? And what of the persistent rule breaker, the recidivist? Do they go to prison? If so, we are almost back to square one. Although less complex than some of the other questions, nonetheless we require answers. Presumably, most legalisers would oppose a severe criminal justice system lest it be tarnished with the same accusations as prohibition, but presumably too they would not want it to be weak lest it loses respect. Some balance would be required based on a tariff but this may not be easy. Would compulsory treatment feature in the sanctions? If so, what additional sanctions would be required for those unwilling to accept treatment? These and numerous similar questions arise whenever a system of law enforcement is required.

Should any groups of persons be separated to receive special attention?

This question is about whether any social groups should be excluded from the legislation, or rather whether any groups should be given preferential consideration. Prohibition makes no distinction – the law applies to all (or almost all), offering no preferential consideration whether to juveniles or others. In contrast, almost all legalisers say that juveniles should not be included in their legalisation programme; rarely do they offer reasons, and rarely do they examine the implications of their decisions. Occasionally, as with prohibition, juveniles are bracketed with people with mental health problems and learning difficulties, thereby following traditional legal procedures, which identify these as vulnerable groups; however, once again the status quo is accepted, or rather not challenged. Yet the decision to exclude juveniles is of considerable significance. A rational drug policy must seek to encompass juveniles within its parameters, one way or another.

What types of commercial system should operate to supply and distribute the drugs?

Again, this is of significance because it determines the system of supply and distribution. The various models offered show how the drugs might be distributed, and also the pitfalls in each model. And again prohibition is presented as creating all the problems, including the way it deals with alcohol. Rarely are the problems of other forms of distribution examined and the limitations discussed. Yet take, for example, the current marketing and sale of non-prescription and prescription drugs, the former sold over the counter through the supermarket model, and the latter sold through the medical model. There are large numbers of customers taking huge quantities of these drugs, so much so that the extent of the problem is probably greater than those taking illicit drugs who are traditionally referred to as the 'drug problem', that is, taking drugs controlled by the 1971 Misuse of Drugs Act. There are large numbers of out-of-control users, produced as much by the specific supply systems as by anything else, but those very supply systems are the ones being advanced by the legalisers. Again, here is another glaring omission in the legalisers' proposals that requires attention.

These five questions should, I suggest, be asked of any rational drug control policy. There are, of course, others but some can be subsumed under the main questions listed here, or are less important, for example: What to do about advertising? How to deal with the media? (The media regularly contribute to drug debates but often in ways that are ill informed and polarised. Once a phrase gets into the media it becomes difficult to change the language.) For the present, these can be left aside. No one pretends that the five questions are easy or straightforward but they ought to be asked nonetheless.

The case against prohibition is made often, and with varying degrees of success. If the proposals examined here are representative of the anti-prohibition stance generally, then in my judgement, they have failed. None has answered satisfactorily the five questions asked above. All in their way have a point to make but none provides a sufficient justification for change. It is not enough to show the defects of an existing system. The case for change has to be made on more authoritative grounds, including detailed considerations of likely failings, and likely consequences. Too often the proposals have been wildly optimistic, and simplistic about implications. This is not an appeal to the status quo but a warning about the dangers of making wrong decisions. I want to return to the statement made at the beginning of Chapter One by Mark Kleiman who, when asked how best to proceed, said that there were things that we could do about drug policy that would reduce the numbers in prison, and the extent of drug abuse and drug-related crime, but legalisation was not one of them. Why? Because he thought that the legalisation debate was a distraction from doing the real work of fixing the drug problem (Kleiman, 2008). I don't think it is a distraction but I do think it should not distract us from other questions that are equally important.

Bibliography

ACMD (Advisory Council on the Misuse of Drugs) (1988) *AIDS and Drug Misuse: Part 1*, London: HMSO.

ACPO (Association of Chief Police Officers) (2008) *ACPO Recommends Cannabis Classification*, press release, 5 February, Ref 11/08, London: ACPO.

Ashton, M. (2003) 'Hepatitis C and needle exchange', *Drug and Alcohol Findings*, no 9.

Ashton, M. (2007) 'The new abstentionists', *Druglink*, vol 18, no 43, pp 1-16.

Bakalar, J. and Grinspoon, L. (1984) *Drug Control in a Free Society*, Cambridge: Cambridge University Press.

Bean, P.T. (1974) *The Social Control of Drugs*, Oxford: Martin Robertson.

Bean, P.T. (1981) *Punishment*, Oxford: Martin Robertson.

Bean, P.T. (1984) *Ecstacy; supply and use*, Report to Business Against Drugs (mimeo).

Bean, P.T. (2006) 'The health of drug users', in J. Goethals, F. Hutsebaut and G. Vervaeke (eds) *Gerechtelijke, Geestelizke Gezondheidszorg*, Leuven: University of Leuven, pp 57-69.

Bean, P.T. (2008) *Drugs and Crime* (3rd edition), Cullompton: Willan Publishing.

Bean, P.T. and Ravenscroft, A. (2004) 'Therapeutic addicts; their treatment and control', in P.T. Bean and T. Nemitz (eds) *Drug Treatment: What Works?* London: Routledge, pp 178-90.

Bean, P.T. and Wilkinson, C.K. (1988) 'Drug taking, crime and the illicit supply system', *British Journal of Addiction*, vol 83, no 5, pp 533-9.

Becker, J. and Roe, S. (2005) *Drug Use among Vulnerable Groups of Young People: Findings from the 2003 Crime and Justice Survey*, London: Home Office.

Bennett, W. (1989) 'Drug policy and the intellectuals', Speech delivered at the Kennedy School of Government, Harvard University, 11 December, mimeo.

Bentham, J. (1948) *An Introduction to the Principles of Morals and Legislation*, Oxford: Basil Blackwell.

Billingsley, R., Nemitz, T. and Bean, P.T. (eds) (2001) *Informers: Policing Policy and Practice*, Cullompton: Willan Publishing.

Brewer, C. (2004) 'Psychological and pharmacological components of treatment', in P.T. Bean and T. Nemitz (eds) *Drug Treatment: What Works?*, London: Routledge, pp 84-109.

Canadian Centre on Substance Abuse Working Group (1996) Mimeo.

Chaiken, J. and Chaiken, M. (1990) 'Drugs and predatory crime', in M. Tonry and J.Q. Wilson (eds) *Drugs and Crime*, Chicago, IL: University of Chicago Press, pp 203-40.

Clarke, R. (2001) 'Informers and corruption', in R. Billingsley, T. Nemitz and P.T. Bean (eds) *Informers: Policing Policy and Practice*, Cullompton: Willan Publishing, pp 38-49.

DH (Department of Health) (2003) *Injectable Heroin and Injectable Methadone: Potential Roles in Drug Treatment*, London: DH.

Dole, M. and Nyswander, V. (1965) 'A medical treatment for diacetylmorphine (heroin) addiction: a clinical trial with methadone hydrochloride', *Journal of the American Medical Association*, vol 193, pp 646-50.

Farrell, M., Ward, J., Mattick, R., Hall, W., Stimson, G.V., des Jarlais, D., Gossop, M. and Strang, J. (1994) 'Methadone maintenance treatment in opiate dependence', *British Medical Journal*, vol 309, pp 997-1101.

Farrington, D.P. (1997) 'Human development and criminal careers', in M. Maguire, R. Morgan and R. Reiner (eds) *The Oxford Handbook of Criminology*, Oxford: Oxford University Press, pp 361-408.

Faugier, J. and Sargeant, M. (1997) 'Boyfriends, "pimps" and clients', in G. Scambler and A. Scambler (eds) *Rethinking Prostitution*, London: Routledge, pp 121-36.

Friedman, M. and Szasz, T. (1992) *On Liberty and Drugs*, Washington, DC: Drug Policy Foundation.

GMC (General Medical Council) (undated) *0 to 18 Years: Guidance for All Doctors*, London: GMC Publications.

Goode, E. (1999) 'Thinking about the drug policy debate', in J. Inciardi (ed) *The Drug Legalisation Debate*, London: Sage Publications, pp 111-24.

Gyngell, G. (2007) *Breakthrough Britain: Ending the Costs of Social Breakdown*, Conservative Social Justice Policy Group.

Hansard (1971) *Misuse of Drugs Bill 1971*, (Also Lord Windelsham), 14 February.

Hawks, D. and Lenton, S. (1995) 'Harm reduction in Australia: has it worked? A review', *Drug and Alcohol Review*, vol 14, pp 291-304.

HM Government (2002) *The Government's Drug Strategy*.

HM Government (2004) *Every Child Matters* (December).

HM Government (2007) *Government Harm Reduction Action Plan* (May). (Also published by the Ministry of Health)

HM Government (2008) *Drugs; Protecting Families and Communities Action Plan* (1st edition).

Home Office (2005) *Drug Offenders in England and Wales* (Findings 256), London: Home Office.

Home Office (2008) (press release) *Government Crackdown on Cannabis*.

House of Commons Home Affairs Committee (2002a) *The Government's Drug Policy: Is it Working?*, Third Report of Session 2001-2002, vol 1, HC 318-1, paras 265-76.

House of Commons Home Affairs Select Committee (2002b) *The Government's Drug Policy: Is it Working?* (The Government's reply to the Third Report from the Home Affairs Committee Session 2001-2002), HC 318, Cm 5573.

Husak, D.N. (1992) *Drugs and Rights*, Cambridge: Cambridge University Press.

Husak, D.N. (1998) 'Two rationales for drug policy: how they shape the content of reform', in J.M. Fish (ed) *How to Legalise Drugs*, New Jersey, NJ: Aronson, pp 29-60.

INCB (International Narcotics Control Board) (2007) *Annual Report*, 1 March, Vienna: INCB.

INCB (2008) *Annual Report*, 5 March, Vienna: INCB (press release relating to that Report 2008).

Inciardi, J. (1989a) 'Legalization; a high risk alternative in the war on drugs', *American Behavioural Scientist*, vol 32, no 3, pp 259-89.

Inciardi, J. (1989b) 'Debating the legalisation of drugs', *American Behavioural Scientist*, vol 32, pp 233-42.

Inciardi, J. (1999) 'Legalising drugs: would it really reduce violent crime?', in J. Inciardi (ed) *The Drug Legalisation Debate* (2nd edition), Thousand Oaks, CA: Sage Publications, pp 55-74.

Inciardi, J. (1990) 'The drugs crime connection', in J. Inciardi (ed) *Handbook of Drug Control in the US*, New York and London: Greenwood Press, pp 71-90.

Inciardi, J. (2000) 'Harm reduction and criminal justice', in J. Inciardi and L. Harrison (eds) *Harm Reduction: National and International Perspectives*, London: Sage Publications, pp 193-206.

Inciardi, J. and Harrison, L. (eds) (2000) *Harm Reduction: National and International Perspectives*, London: Sage Publications.

Inciardi, J. and McBride, D.C. (1989) 'Legalisation: a high risk alternative', *American Behavioural Scientist*, vol 32, no 3, pp 259-89.

Inciardi, J. and McBride, D.C. (1990) 'Debating the legalisation of drugs', in J. Inciardi (ed) *Handbook of Drug Control in the US*, New York and London: Greenwood Press, pp 283-99.

Inciardi, J. and McBride, D. (1991) 'The case against legalisation', in J. Inciardi (ed) *The Drug Legalisation Debate*, London: Sage Publications, pp 45-79.

Inciardi, J., Lockwood, D. and Pottieger, A. (1993) *Women and Crack Cocaine*, London: Macmillan.

International Harm Reduction Association (1996) *What is Harm Reduction?*, London: IHRA.

International Harm Reduction Association (2008) *Global State of Harm Reduction*, London: IHRA, p 119. [See also Gerry Stimson in his introductory comments of that edition.]

Jacobs, J. (1990) 'Imagining drug legalisation', *The Public Interest*, vol 101, pp 28-42.

Karel, R. (1991) 'A model legalisation proposal', in J. Inciardi (ed) *The Drug Legalisation Debate* (2nd edition), Thousand Oaks, CA: Sage Publications, pp 80-102.

Kleber, H.D. and Inciardi, J. (2005) 'Clinical and societal implications of drug legalisation', in J.H. Lowinson (ed) *Substance Abuse: A Comprehensive Textbook* (4th edition), Baltimore, MD: Williams and Wilkins, pp 1383-1400.

Kleiman, M. (1993) Letter to *The Economist*, 12-18 June, p 8.

Kleiman, M. (2008) 'Arguments for and against drug prohibition', (quoted by Morgan, S. and posted in Chronicle Blog 18 Feb 2008) Wikipedia website.

Kleiman, M. and Saiger, A.J. (1990) 'Drug legalisation: the importance of asking the right question', *Hofstra Law Review*, vol 18, no 3 (A Symposium on Drug Decriminalisation), pp 527-65.

Levi, M. and Osofsky, L. (1995) *Investigating, Seizing and Confiscating the Proceeds of Crime*, London: Home Office, Police Research Group.

Levi, M. and Reuter, P. (2006) 'Money laundering', in M. Tonry (ed) *Crime and Justice: An Annual Review of Research*, Chicago, IL: University of Chicago Press, pp 289-375.

Levine, R. (1993) 'Medicalisation of psychoactive substance abuse', in R. Bayer and G.M. Oppenheimer (eds) *Confronting Drug Policy*, Cambridge: Cambridge University Press, pp 319-36.

Liberty (2001) *The Government's Drug Policy. Is it working?* Submission to Home Affairs Select Committee, September.

Lipton, D.S. (1989) *The Theory of Rehabilitation as Applied to Addict Offenders*, Mimeo.

Lowinson, J.H. (2005) *Substance Misuse: A Comprehensive Textbook* (4th edition), Baltimore, MD: Williams and Wilkins.

MacCoun, R., Kelmer, B. and Reuter, P. (2002) *Research on Drugs and Crime Linkages*, Mimeo.

Matrix Knowledge Group (2007) *The Illicit Drug Trade in the UK*, Online Report 20/07, London: Home Office.

May, T., Edmunds, M., Hough, M. and Harvey, C. (1999) *Street Business: The Links between Sex and Drug Markets*, Police Research Series Paper No 118, London: Home Office.

McBride, D.C., Terry, Y.M. and Inciardi, J. (1999) 'Alternative perspectives on the drug policy debate', in J. Inciardi (ed) *The Drug Legalisation Debate*, London: Sage Publications, pp 9-54.

McKegany, N. (2008) 'Should heroin be prescribed to heroin users? No', *British Medical Journal*, vol 336, p 71.

McSweeney, T., Turnball, P. and Hough, M. (2008) *Tackling Drug Markets and Distribution Networks in the UK*, Institute of Criminal Policy Review, London: King's College London.

McVay, D. (1992) 'Marijuana legalisation: the time is now', in J. Inciardi (ed) *The Legalisation Debate*, London: Sage Publications, pp 147-60.

Mill, J.S. (1946) *On Liberty*, Blackwell, (Everyman Edition)

Miller, N. and Gold, M. (1994) 'Criminal activity and crack addiction', *International Journal of Addictions*, vol 29, no 8, pp 1065-81.

Ministry of Health (1926) *Departmental Committee on Morphine and Heroin Addiction Report* (The Rolleston Report).

Ministry of Health and Scottish Home and Health Department (1965) *Drug addiction; the second report of the Interdepartmental Committee* (The second Brain Report).

Moore, M. (1984) 'Regulating heroin: Kaplan and Trebach on the dilemmas of public policy', *American Bar Foundation Research Journal*, pp 723-31.

Moore, M. (1992a) 'Actually prohibition was a success', in R.L. Evans and I.M. Berent (eds) *Drug Legalisation: For and Against*, La Salle, CA: Open Court Publications, pp 95-7.

Moore, M. (1992b) 'Drugs: getting a fix on the problem and solution', in R.L. Evans and I.M. Berent (eds) *Drug Legalisation: For and Against*, La Salle, CA: Open Court Publications, pp 123-55.

Nadelmann, E.A. (1991) 'The case for legalisation', in J. Inciardi (ed) *The Drug Legalisation Debate*, London: Sage Publications, pp 17-44.

Nadelmann, E.A. (1992) 'Thinking seriously about alternatives to drug prohibition', *Daedalus*, vol 121, pp 87-132.

Nadelmann, E.A. (1995) 'Drug prohibition in the United States: costs consequences and alternatives', in J. Inciardi and K. McElrath (eds) *The American Drug Scene*, Los Angeles, CA: Roxbury, pp 322-35.

Nadelmann, E.A. (1999a) 'Common sense drug policy', in J. Inciardi (ed) *The Drug Legalisation Debate* (2nd edition), London: Sage Publications, pp 157-72.

Nadelmann, E. (1999b) 'The case for legalisation', in J. Inciardi (ed) *The Drug Legalisation Debate* (2nd edition), London: Sage Publications, pp 17-44.

Neyroud, P. and Beckley, A. (2001) 'Regulating informers: RIPA covert policing and human rights', in R. Billingsley, T. Nemitz and P.T. Bean (eds) *Informers: Policing Policy and Practice*, Cullompton: Willan Publishing, pp 164-75.

NTA (National Treatment Agency) (2003a) *Research into Practice Briefing No 2: Prescribing Services for Drug Misuse*, January, NTA, Mimeo, www.nta.nhs.uk/publications/documents/nta_prescribing_services_drug_misuse_2003_rip2.pdf

NTA (2003b) *Injectable Heroin and Injectable Methadone in Drug Treatment*, London: NTA.

Ostrowski, J. (1990) 'The moral and practical case for drug legalisation', *Hofstra Law Review*, vol 18, no 3 (A Symposium on Drug Decriminalisation), pp 607-702.

Pauly, B. (2008) 'Harm reduction through a social justice lens', *International Journal of Drug Policy*, vol 19, no 1, pp 4-10.

Platt, A. (1969) *The Child Savers: The Invention of Delinquency*, Chicago, IL: University of Chicago Press.

Reuter, P. (1992) 'Hawks ascendant: the punitive trend of American drug policy', *Daedalus*, vol 121, pp 15-52.

Reuter, P. and MacCoun, R. (1996) 'Harm reduction and social policy', *Drug and Alcohol Review*, vol 15, pp 225-30.

Reuter, P. and Stevens, A. (2007) *An Analysis of UK Drug Policy*: UK Drug Policy Commission.

Reuter, P., Farrell, M. and Strang, J. (1994) 'The non-case for legalisation', in R. Stevenson (ed) *Winning the War on Drugs: To Legalise or Not?*, Hobart Paper No 124, Commentary (2), London: Institute of Economic Affairs, pp 83-90.

Sanders, T. (2005) *Sex Work: A Risky Business*, Cullompton: Willan Publishing.

Schmoke, K.L. (1990) 'An argument in favour of decriminalisation', *Hofstra Law Review*, vol 18, no 3 (A Symposium on Drug Decriminalisation), pp 501-25.

Schuler, J.T. and McBride, A. (1990) 'Notes from the front: a dissident law-enforcement perspective on drug prohibition', *Hofstra Law Review*, vol 18, no 3 (A Symposium on Drug Decriminalisation), pp 893-942.

Spear, H.B. (2002) (Edited by Joy Mott) *Heroin Addiction, Care and Control*, London: Drugscope.

Stevenson, R. (1994) *Winning the War on Drugs: To Legalise or Not?*, Hobart Paper No 124, London: Institute of Economic Affairs.

Stimson, G.V. (2007) 'Harm reduction – coming of age', *International Journal of Drug Policy*, vol 18, no 2, pp 67-9.

Szasz, T. (1996) *Our Right to Use Drugs: The Case for a Free Market*, Syracuse, NY: Syracuse University Press.

Thornton, M. (1998) 'Perfect drug legalisation', in J.M. Fish (ed) *How to Legalise Drugs*, New Jersey, NJ: Aronson, pp 638-60.

Transform (2005) *Illegal Drugs: The Problem is Prohibition, the Solution is Control and Regulation*, Bristol: Transform Drug Policy Foundation.

Transform (2006) *After the War on Drugs: Options for Control*, Bristol: Transform.

Transform (2007) *After the War on Drugs: Tools for the Debate*, Bristol: Transform.

Trebach, A. and Inciardi, J. (eds) (1993) *Legalise It? Debating American Drug Policy*, Washington, DC: American University Press.

UN (United Nations) General Assembly (2006) *Political Declaration on HIV/AIDS*: UN, pp 1-6.

UNODC (United Nations Office on Drugs and Crime) (2007) *World Drug Report* (December).

West, D.J. and Farrington, D. (1977) *The Delinquent Way of Life*, London: Routledge and Kegan Paul.

Wilson, J.Q. (1995) 'Against the legalisation of drugs', in J. Inciardi and K. McElrath (eds) *The American Drug Scene*, Los Angeles, CA: Roxbury, pp 336-44.

Wootton, B. (1968) *Cannabis*, Report by the Advisory Committee on Drug Dependence, London: HMSO.

Yandle, B. (1983) 'Bootleggers and Baptists: the education of a regulatory economist', *Regulation* 7, no 3, p 12.

Name and subject index